LAST CUT

SAMANTHA PAIGE

Photographs by LISA FIELD

LAST CUT ™

Photographs by Lisa Field (unless otherwise noted)
Book and cover design by Rafael Pulido
Editing by Jennifer Pooley, Nancy Tan, and Adetayo West

ISBN 978-1-7336049-4-9 (hardcover)
ISBN 978-1-7336049-9-4 (paperback)

Published by Last Cut, LLC
www.lastcutproject.com

Printed on FSC-certified paper by Paper Chase Press in Los Angeles, California

This book is dedicated to my daughter. I love you to the moon and back and back again infinitely.

In memory of Kathryn Knowles and Yuri Angela Chung. Cancer took you both from us too soon, but your strength, wisdom, and love live on in my heart.

I would like to acknowledge that many of my experiences, both physical and emotional, were lived through a lens of privilege as a white woman living in the United States of America. This does not minimize my personal trauma but recognizes a more general comfort. I had good insurance coverage, either through my parents or because I could afford it. I had a supportive family. I had resources to pay for therapy and to make changes—sometimes radical ones—in my life. In stating this, I note that some of the last cuts I have shared may have been afforded by this privilege.

I believe in the importance of a deep commitment to last cut living, which is a state of mind that makes us question all the principles we were told are the golden rules to happiness. This is a way of being that questions the status quo, which seeks to tell us there is one right way. At any given moment, we might not have the ability to throw it all out the window or to step into something new, but there is great power in the internal shifts that motivate us to stand up for ourselves and others in profoundly life-changing ways.

"I see in myself, Lucilius, not just an improvement but a transformation, although I would not venture as yet to assure you, or even to hope, that there is nothing left in me needing to be changed. Naturally there are a lot of things about me requiring to be built up or fined down or eliminated. Even this, the fact that it perceives the failings it was unaware of in itself before, is evidence of a change for the better in one's character."

—SENECA, *Letters from a Stoic*

One of the affordances of social media platforms is their potential to connect people and their ability to encourage a unified feeling of community through these connections. Like many, Sam and I became aware of each other on social media; we connected and then quickly became friends outside that realm. Social media is the most powerful when it brings strangers together through the stories they tell. Digital storytelling nowadays motivates us to act and *react*. Like Sam and me with our stories, though different, the words we shared were our naked truths, speaking on taboo subjects such as illness, scars, fear, pain, shame, and how we find strength in our vulnerabilities; and that honesty is what drew us to each other. Through *Last Cut Project*, Sam was documenting and exploring her road to self-recovery and self-discovery. She was sharing her aches and pains and struggles and loss with the world, and was doing so with complete *sincerity*, with just her words, her self-portraits, her body, and just by revealing her *self*, uncut and uncensored—all the while destigmatizing these things that lack conversation. When I first came across *Last Cut Project*, it was invigorating and inspiring to see someone be so raw and unafraid to reveal her whole self by disregarding all the taboos and

breaking the mold. I had seen and read a ton on breast reconstruction after cancer, but I had never known anything about reversing the procedure, nor the word for the operation: "explant." She was telling *her truth* as I was trying to do the same.

I began writing *Notes to a Friend* shortly after my cancer recurrence in 2015. It was my way of coping with my pain and fear, and it eventually became my road to healing and an essential way of holding on to myself while trying to understand my new self. I imagine that *Last Cut Project* has been a similar journey for Sam as *Notes to a Friend* has been for me. I never would've imagined that my words would reach so many people—people who I realized needed my notes, needed to hear the truths about metastatic breast cancer beyond the pink ribbons and medical facts, and *needed* to know that they are not alone in this abyss. It didn't take long for Sam and me to become friends. Our individual stories shared so many parallels. We saw each other. We saw the other's pains and truths. Essentially, we became a witness to each other's lives; sometimes all you need is to be seen and heard to heal. The more we share these truths with each other, and the more connections we make through

these truths, the better we can help each
other heal. Every connection we make
is no accident. Sam and I spoke of the
stars aligning for our entrances into
each other's lives. I truly believe that
we are all here on our paths to serve a
greater purpose than just ourselves. I am
honored to have a place in Sam's life and
story. And I am certain that her bravery,
generosity, and willingness to share her
most intimate trials and tribulations
have touched many others along the
way and believe *Last Cut Project* will
continue to heal lost souls—*just as she
has mended mine.*

by YURI ANGELA CHUNG of *Notes
to a Friend*

7.16.18

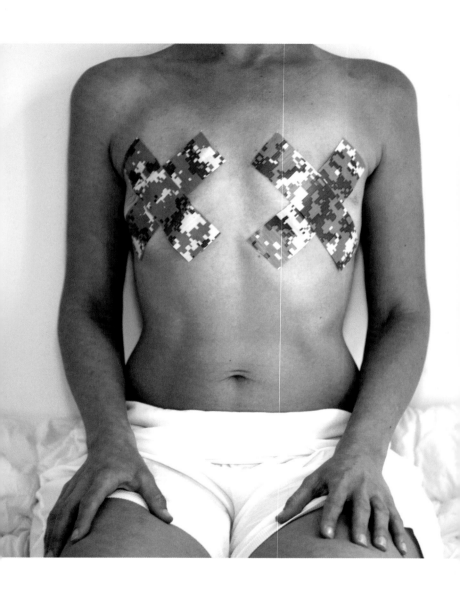

On January 22, 2016, I walked into the sixth major surgery of my life, to remove my silicone implants. I would like to believe this significant life decision—or last cut, as I like to call these moments, will be the last surgery I face. It certainly has been the most impactful. As I reflect on that day, what is worthy of celebration is not solely the massive improvement in my physical health (which has far exceeded any hopes or expectations I had going into that operation), but the power of lining up my internal beliefs with my actions in the world. This particular last cut was a watershed moment for me in my personal life. My individual embodiment, though, is compounded by how this one decision grew into *Last Cut Project*, which in turn created a community around bold, brave empowerment beyond my story that is strengthening every day.

I never could have predicted how 2016 would roll out after choosing the word "embodiment" as my intention on New Year's Eve. The literal physical embodiment I have experienced, as well as the fulfillment of my mission to create conversation and community around truth, has far exceeded my wildest dreams.

My personal choice to act on behalf of what was most true to me in that given moment was made with a simultaneous dedication to attach words and imagery to a process we all experience over and over in life. There is a universal thread in any last cut moment that connects us beyond the details of any one of our stories. We have experienced moments in which we feel like strangers in our own lives. In some place within ourselves or out in the world, we know what it is to sense incongruence between what we feel and what we do. These are the moments when we have the power to elicit change. These are the times when we can boldly and bravely act on behalf of our truths to do what is possible to set ourselves free and help support others in doing the same.

There is no one last cut in any of our lives. Every "last" cut is a desire that this single action will set us free. If I quit this job, I will be happy. If I leave or step into this marriage, I will feel whole. The list of wistful conditions is long. Yet, we live in a dynamic world. Everything within and around us is constantly evolving. We have a choice as to whether we dedicate ourselves to staying on the pulse of that change so that, to the best of our abilities and circumstances, we are matching up our values with our actions. No one day, no one action, is last and final. True freedom and growth occur when we commit to this philosophy as a way of being. When we take an oath to continually ask ourselves, "What is most true to me in this moment?" and "How am I living that truth in this moment?" and take action when called for, we begin to live the change we seek in the world around us.

One day that might be the decision to remove your silicone implants, if resources and an internal calling to do so collide, and tomorrow it may be

"I was embarrassed and full of shame when I had an MRSA staph infection for six months before my explant surgery. The infection hurt like hell, and the lesions that covered my upper torso and neck were outright disgusting to me. I cleared that beast leading up to the operation, yet still cringe when I feel the scar tissue along the back of my neck. Instead of saying unkind words to myself when I trace those bumps, I correct myself and choose to remember how that infection led me to now."

standing up for the rights of millions to have access to health care, fair treatment by the police or equitable access to housing and education. One day that might be picking up the phone or writing letters to your congressional leaders, voicing your opinion on what you desire to change. It may be informing yourself of upcoming opportunities to vote, get involved, support, speak up, and advocate on behalf of your own rights or those of others. It may be speaking up to a bully or coaching your child to do so. It may be realizing the ways you are being a bully to yourself or others and altering those behaviors. Perhaps you are in an unhappy relationship? Perhaps you are not being treated well by your partner? Perhaps you are not treating your partner well? Whatever it looks like, there is never a last opportunity to speak up, stand up, and act on behalf of yourself and others who need your support.

The desire to be an open, vulnerable, and connected human is why I am doing this. I am writing and engaging, not because I have all the answers, but because I want to learn a better way. I want to connect, because I strongly believe that by asking the hard questions of each other and listening to the answers with an open mind and heart, we can heal. The ability to share what is most true to you and know you are being seen and heard is where magic happens. This open connection sparks clarity, action, and foundational strength. Being seen and feeling whole inspire us to continue to show up for ourselves and for each other. It is for that reason I started the *Last Cut Conversations* podcast, and it is for that reason I am sharing my story. Sometimes we have to dig deeper and look further for the answers we seek. Those connections fuel more love and resolve, which further our ability to participate more fully and consciously in life. And in this rocky and unpredictable world, those bonds and the growth they foster provide a welcome glimmer of hope.

My Story

Allowing myself to change authentically has been the most
powerful agent of healing and growth in my life.

5.17.17

"Cancer was the best thing that ever happened to me."

These words elicit a strong reaction from most cancer survivors and patients. Many in the C-word camp will tell you how much they despise hearing how cancer was a gift. Certainly no one would wish cancer, as an instigator of change or catalyst for self-reflection, upon another. Yet, when we are battling the disease, we are told to put on our armor, be strong, and fight back with a smile. Moving directly to this place of strength and optimism can often deprive us of the time and space needed to feel the full spectrum of emotions, which are essential to lasting wellness, happiness, and freedom.

What I have personally experienced, as a cancer survivor and previvor,* are some of the most challenging moments in my life, and they have offered me the most profound opportunities for personal growth and change. However, these so-called gifts came in time and with a hefty amount of dedicated

*"Cancer previvors are individuals who are survivors of a predisposition to cancer but who haven't had the disease. This group includes people who have a hereditary mutation, a family history of cancer, or some other predisposing factor. The term specifically applies to the portion of our community that has its own unique needs and concerns separate from the general population, but different from those already diagnosed with cancer." (Facing Our Risk of Cancer Empowered, facingourrisk.org)

self-reflection, healing, and work on my part.

I certainly was not aware of the transformational power of cancer while fighting the disease, as I was wholly focused on surviving and moving forward with my life. I realized only years later that some of my most important life lessons were to be taken from that period in time. The learning and healing were discovered through later self-inquiry and experience, and pulled from the tapestry of my post-cancer life.

In fact, nearly a decade after my illness was when I finally began to cope with the trauma of what had happened to me, and, through the healing process that ensued, I began to make a series of last cuts, or significant decisions, that led to my present well-being and the beginning of *Last Cut Project*, a multimedia documentary project.

In August 1996, I was diagnosed with thyroid cancer at age twenty-one. I had just returned home to Los Angeles from studying abroad in Italy and was getting ready for my senior year of college at Tufts University, when out of the blue my gynecologist happened to feel a lump in my throat during a routine exam. I had spent the prior spring semester studying art history and Italian in Rome. Italian came fairly naturally for me, and I savored the independence and opportunity to live in a foreign country to learn, travel, and explore. Hoping to postpone my return to the United States, I managed to convince my mother to support my desire to spend the beginning of the summer in an intensive Italian language program in Siena. I spent eight hours a day in class and enjoyed dreamy evenings with my local friends and Italian boyfriend. When I returned to the States, bronzed, fluent, and ready for my final academic year of college, my plans were to write my thesis, connect with my dear friends, and explore my next steps in life. They were all derailed by the the the shocking news: "The tumor is malignant."

Prior to my diagnosis, I had never felt better. I had no symptoms and felt full of life and wellness after my time living in Italy. I had found my voice and independence and was completely blindsided by this turn of events. My physical health was not something I had much considered previously, and cancer was certainly not on my radar or in the plan.

In the months that followed, I lived at home with my mom and stepfather. Unpacking my bags in my childhood home instead of my college rental with my roommates created immense heartache. I loved my family, but being back home again in the twin bed of my youth deflated my spirits. All of my excitement and momentum for the year ahead was squashed by overwhelming sadness as my days were now filled with cancer treatment. My thyroid was removed, and I underwent two rounds of radioactive iodine therapy to ensure any remaining malignant cells were annihilated. I longed to be back at college with my friends and in my classes, where I was most content. Instead, my days passed slowly, with the focus on doctors' appointments and healing. My family was kind and supportive, but I ached to be a healthy, carefree college student thousands of miles away from home.

I put forth my best effort to be happy and optimistic, but I was inwardly depressed and passed many hours crying alone in my bedroom. Because I so deeply yearned to be well for myself and the loved ones around me, I hid the painful emotions, always doing my best to keep smiling and functioning. My surgery was successful, and after I healed and endured one round of radioactive iodine treatment, I returned to Tufts to finish college and graduate. I had tried to complete my senior thesis in African studies, but after a few too many failed attempts to get myself to the UCLA library to do research, I was forced to drop the project. As I had been off campus at that point for a year, the administration stipulated that I complete a session of summer school before qualifying for graduation. Yet, having all the required credits completed, I petitioned the academic dean. With my solid grades and some compassion for my recent dance with cancer, I was granted permission to graduate on time and with my class.

Following graduation, I decided to go back to Italy. I found a three-month internship at the Lorenzo de' Medici Institute (LdM) in Florence. After a second round of radioactive iodine treatment just weeks after graduation, I packed my bags and moved back to Italy to work in the school's marketing department for cooking and travel programs and as an ESL teacher for Italians. I figured I would find my way back to some sense of normalcy in the place I loved most.

This began a period of disconnect in my life that would go on for years, until I finally faced the layered ways I had become a stranger in my own life in order to avoid facing the unhealed trauma.

Throughout my twenties, I lived in wonderful cities like Florence, Bologna, and Washington, D.C., working at LdM, pursuing a graduate degree in international studies, and working as an assistant to a fellow at an economic research think tank. I perpetually kept myself doing in order to avoid feeling.

My days were filled with stimulating work and study, but my nights were progressively overtaken with paralyzing anxiety. Sadness, fear, and disappointment had been denied access during my cancer experience, but in time, all three, and many of their friends, demanded a seat at the table. They crept in at night and soon infiltrated my days by way of depression, panic attacks, and chronic, debilitating migraine headaches. I found myself on multiple prescription medications in order to mitigate the paralyzing effects of my inner turmoil, so as to show up at all in life.

Somewhere in the midst of this period, I opted to be tested for the BRCA gene because of my own cancer at age twenty-one and my mother's (successful) breast cancer bout at age thirty-one.

I tested positive for the BRCA1 mutation, which indicates elevated risk of breast and other cancers. This privileged diagnosis triggered a deeper wave of angst around my body and health that shadowed the latter part of my twenties. Cancer's shocking presence in my life years before made me fear another diagnosis was looming with every mammogram, MRI, and follow-up doctor's visit. My life became riddled with migraines, panic attacks, and debilitating anxiety. My ability to function diminished.

Finally, at age twenty-eight, when the nearly daily emergency-room-worthy migraines forced me to claim disability leave from my job, there was no denying that any attempt to live a full and fulfilled life was being thwarted by my untouched trauma. Seven years after my cancer diagnosis, I had no idea what the future would look like for me if I remained on all the prescription medications that seemed to be keeping me afloat. I was disconnected but aware something had to change.

In the years that followed, I dove into ongoing therapy in order to heal and began to approach my health from a more holistic angle. I met a man and got married. We moved from New York

City to Santa Barbara and soon were expecting our first baby.

My daughter's long and challenging birth was a gift. Even with late-onset preeclampsia, I was able to deliver her without a Cesarean section. This harrowing, yet ultimately joyous, experience brought me back into positive dialogue with my body. She brought me a renewed will to find wellness and well-being and a regained trust that my body would not always fail me. I no longer wished to live a disconnected existence ruled by fear.

Within months after her birth, I opted for a preventive double mastectomy and breast reconstruction with silicone implants. At the time, reconstruction was presented as the norm, and I did not listen to the voice inside me whispering that perhaps there were more questions to ask of myself and my doctor. I desired to be free of the frequent and anxiety-ridden testing the BRCA mutation required and simultaneously began to write about the prior ten years of my life. I found emotional and mental relief by processing my physical pain and struggles through words. My hope was that one day these reflections could be shared through a book that would help others feel less alone in their own trials.

Framing the learning I had done—from the thyroid cancer through the preventive double mastectomy—into chapters of a book helped me create structure and space to process my fears, anxieties, and also hopes. Little did I know that years later, the writing and the process I used to formulate order out of inner chaos would plant seeds for the birth of *Last Cut Project*.

Looking back on my cancer experience, I knew the only way to embody happiness was to unpack and heal past pain and trauma. I no longer could distract myself with intellectualizing and busyness. The time had come to go within and heal.

For the nearly eight years following my preventive double mastectomy, I began to do the internal work that would ultimately become the focus of *Last Cut Project*. I started asking myself the straightforward, honest questions I had been avoiding for years. Deep self-inquiry and raw black-and-white dialogue became my way of life, and in time, that inner clarity bled out into my external actions.

I made a series of last cuts that created greater consistency in who I knew I was and how I desired to live my life.

I got a divorce.

I closed Adesso, the jewelry company I had successfully built but fallen out of love with. Adesso had been born from my love of making jewelry as a form of meditation and creative expression. After a lifetime of collecting beads and combining them into designs, I had started doing so as a small business when my daughter was two years old. In time, the business grew beyond my own hands. I hired other local women who helped me make the creations and built a wholesale and retail operation. Years into this endeavor, I recognized that what was an external success in many ways was no longer fueling my soul or creativity.

I had a full hysterectomy.

I sold the house we lived in as a family of three and moved with my daughter to our first post-divorce home together just a few blocks down.

I walked away from another serious relationship because of incongruent values.

Through all of these life changes, I recognized the importance of internal dialogue, honesty with myself about the answers, action where I needed to live a more fulfilled, connected life, and a like-minded community.

After clearing away so much, I was able to recognize my silicone implants were another place where my internal and external worlds were no longer consistent.

In January 2016, I was privileged to be in a position to opt for an explant surgery to remove the implants I had elected with my preventive double mastectomy in 2008. *Last Cut Project* was born from a desire to capture the physical artistically and to create community and conversation around these moments of notable change. From the day I decided to have that surgery, I committed to writing about the physical and emotional and everything in between as I healed. Lisa Field, a photographer and my dear friend, agreed to capture this important moment in my life by taking pictures of me as I traversed yet another significant medical event. While *Last Cut Project* began as a story told through my words and Lisa's imagery about my personal life, it soon became apparent that the story of my decision to explant was a perfect metaphor for these universal moments in which we seek to create greater congruency between our inner and outer worlds. Months into the creation of *Last Cut Project*, the podcast *Last Cut Conversations* was born, and the dialogue extended beyond my chest and reached out to many through words, photography, and discourse.

While most last cuts are internal jobs, we are able to move and heal with greater ease, grace, and bravery when we know we are not alone. I learned the importance of support and community by living through a series of massive last cuts in a short span of time and desired to speak with others about their last cut moments. Looking back, I wish I had known the importance of having raw, honest conversation about every shift in life, especially the challenging ones. It is not that there is always beauty in the painful, but there is tremendous value in taking the time to work through these experiences.

A decade after my cancer diagnosis was when I finally began to garner what thyroid cancer had to offer. In the short term, I adopted the socially acceptable lesson to live life fully, embrace the moment, and savor the beauty—but truly embodying those adages did not come until much later and through much more suffering.

As I trace over the events and moments from my cancer diagnosis at age twenty-one to the present, I see how inner pain caused me to turn my back on what I knew to be true. The consequences of yeses that should have been noes have rattled every corner of my being and remembering. I knew in my body and overrode with my mind. I have lived fully and without regret. I live today with humility and reverence for how the body knows and guides.

After twenty years of struggling with maintaining my health, I began to wonder if wellness, wholeness, and freedom in my body were the stuff of dreams. Before my explant surgery, I held such sincere and deep hopes that removing my implants would foster better health and greater life in my body. Yet, I never know until I am on the other side of these trials what the outcome will be.

What I learned in the long run is there is no fast track to optimism and happiness. The road is often long, but when we feel all the feelings and do the internal work, we find deeper connection and lasting happiness, wellness, and freedom. If we own the often less embraced emotions—the ones deemed by society to be negative and lesser—and feel all the emotions through to make space for beauty, levity, and lasting growth, we create space to welcome in whatever is happening in the present moment without the constant filter of our trauma.

Reminding ourselves we do not have to do the healing alone provides great relief, as community in these last cut moments offers support and strength.

As I discovered with *Last Cut Project* at age forty-one, twenty years after my cancer diagnosis, we never know what doors a painful experience will open, but the surest way to find out is to stay in the conversation with yourself and others.

What is a last cut?

What Is a Last Cut?

Vulnerable truth is powerful medicine.

11.23.16

Last cuts speak to owning the truth of each experience we have and bravely and honestly seeing it through until it sets us free. Our (internal/external) scars become the most beautiful reflections of who we are.

11.16.16

Last cuts are the ongoing decisions we make in life—a walking toward what we desire more of or a stepping away from that which is no longer working. Making a last cut is often about notable change. Sometimes these shifts happen within one's own life, and other times, a decision made by one affects many. No matter the scale, these last cut moments require a tremendous amount of bravery to create more freedom.

2.6.18

Last Cut Project is about those big life decisions made to bring us closer to living greater truth and freedom.

1.18.17

Every time I tell my story and hear the stories of others out in the world, I heal, change, and grow. Storytelling may be one of the oldest forms of communication and connection and, I would argue, the most transformative. A whole new world reveals itself through each fresh telling of a story, even the ones we've told many times and will continue to tell.

12.27.17

"We make the best decisions we can in every moment based on the information we have." My mom has

"We actually have the capacity to heal ourselves even if it's just by sharing our story. If I share my story and then I pass the baton to you to share your story, then you're healing yourself. I've just sparked the remembrance in you that you have that capacity."

—MELINDA ALEXANDER, author of *Getting Free: A Love Story*

"It also becomes my responsibility to let that emotion flow through me so that it says, 'Hey, I see you.' As I am emotional, as I open myself up, I allow other people to open themselves up too. As I allow myself to be seen, I'm doing the same thing for my audience. In that way, we're no longer alone and we're no longer cursed. We see we're not that different after all."

—MONIQUE MITCHELL, poet, Head of Community Outreach
for Get Lit, and youth mentor

repeated that sentiment to me over and over throughout my life. The key is to continue asking the truthful questions and keep facing the honest answers. With a dose of (self-)kindness along the way, I now can look myself in the mirror with peace and happiness.

5.26.17

I am not sure if a story is ever fully done or if it simply blends into and informs the next one. There are clear completions and beginnings that happen, which is certainly at the heart of *Last Cut Project*. However, the way every story becomes a part of who we are and what comes next is a rather fluid and amorphous state of affairs.

12.28.17

Feeling well on all levels starts from within us, and in my opinion, we feel best and most free when our external actions are an extension of our own unique inner world.

1.23.17

These cracked-open moments of truth are where change happens.

7.15.16

A last cut brings more openings.
A last cut brings more lightness.
A last cut brings more illumination.
A last cut brings more solidity.
A last cut brings more magic.

3.28.16

I feel like a stranger
in my own life

Disconnect

We all have experienced feeling like a stranger in our own lives. We have woken up and looked around at the life we have created—the decisions we have made—only to wonder how we got there. This moment of recognition that who we are on the inside is not matching up with the decisions we have made outside in the world is the first, and quite fundamental, step in making a last cut. We must first identify what does not feel right, on our own, before we can remedy the disconnect we feel. We must give name to the uneasiness, pain, hope, or desire before we can determine how to find ways to enact change. This phase of making a last cut is often the most difficult. It can be far easier to uphold the illusion that nothing is wrong, to continue with old patterns that may have served us in the past and preserve the status quo. However, tolerance of what is not working holds us back from exploring a life that does feel like our own and separates us from the possibility for greater happiness, wellness, and freedom.

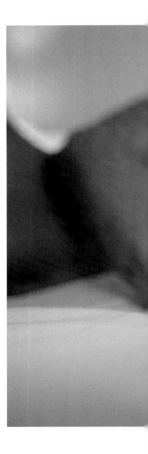

My body is my greatest teacher. Truth lives in the body, and the body doesn't lie. So I trust the messages I receive through my physical experience. When I feel something off in my body, I pay attention and ask questions about how I am navigating my life.

10.19.17

"I've learned to treat my emotions now as teachers. I feel as if they have arisen in me to teach me either something about what I'm experiencing, something about the past, or something about myself."

—MONIQUE MITCHELL

We must strip things down.
We must ask questions.
We must face the (often ugly) truths.

2.15.17

"We are all so much more than what we can see."

—VANESSA CUCCIA
Founder of Chakrubs

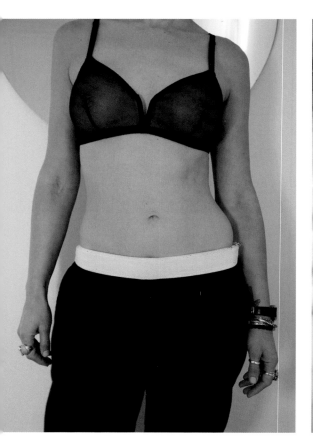 

I do not want to settle for the imposition of anyone else's beliefs on how I should look, feel, or identify. If I settle, I am quietly and passively saying okay to something that is not right and allowing it to fester.

7.28.16

The things I believe identify or define me are often the paralyzing
blocks to my happiness and well-being.

10.28.16

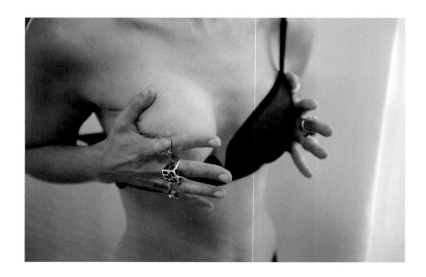

i search for the right words,
to describe the sensations,
that do not feel as if they belong,
in my body,
in my mind,
as if a (proper) phrase might offer relief,
or resolution?
perhaps i do better
to remain in the quiet
and walk with the feeling.

10.29.17

I think often of yeses that should have been noes. I recall the times I wish I would have said no instead of yes, and vice versa. There were times when I went along with something because I thought it would be good or right for me. Other times, I knew better and still agreed.

3.5.18

If I don't pay attention, life can get in the way and disconnect me from the very things that keep me going and make me feel whole.

12.6.17

Floating in a space where confusion has found clarity, but action has yet to show desired results; there is simply observation of what is.

11.13.17

Why do I torture myself?
I walk up this hot, dry, sinking hill time and time again.
Where do I think it will lead?
I dress myself up and hope to experience something different than before.
I can see fully in every direction.
Every rock.
Every plant.
Every slope.
No shade left untouched by the hot, blazing sun.
There is no mystery here.
The landscape is an open book.
Yet my hope leads me back to that hill once again.
I show up with my suitcase of dreams, wishes, expectations, and desires.
I've packed my best intentions.
I am ready to stay, but there is no availability.
All booked.
I have dreamt of and yearned for a beautiful oasis, but it is never there.
There is dryness as far as my eye can see.
When will I realize (learn/honor/value/respect myself/know) that it is time to walk the other way?
I know there is (water/ice/food/drink/love/shelter/friendship/truth/honesty/depth/respect/reciprocity/love)
just across the way.
They (I) are (am) ready to welcome (see/honor/respect/hear/meet) me.
So I turn and go.
Today.

I have continued to climb the same hill to nowhere. I expect that the trek will be worth the struggle each new time. I naively set out to face the sinking sand, the blazing rays of the sun, and the radiating heat one more time. It will be different this time, yet somewhere deep inside me, I have known there is no oasis at the top of this hill. So why do I return to try again and again in search of some shady, welcoming spot to rest and share? Why don't I turn and walk in another direction? The wind blows and brings voice of other lands where there is welcome and sustenance. Where do I want to go? How do I want to feel? How do I show myself respect? How do I care for my own health and well-being? Where does hope meet reality? Where does reality meet what I desire? When do I need to walk in a different direction? I have learned this lesson before. I have been provided with a clear map. I know the way. It is a choice, and only mine to make.

9.6.16

The more I said no to that which was not mine, the more I found my true yes.

6.19.17

For far too long, I lived my life constricted by the vision of the person I thought I should be. I held back. I hid. I filtered. I forgot. I numbed. I pleased others over my own well-being. I shunned my own uniqueness for more acceptable societal mores. I minimized my own voice for fear of not being lovable in my real state. I gave my power over to guilt. I betrayed myself and tolerated others betraying me. These ways of being made me sick. I became a (trapped) stranger in my own life. I decided to change. I stepped out of the box and owned who I am. I slowly found my way back to freedom, one last cut at a time.

9.22.17

What matters most to me?

Questioning

The way forward from a state of disconnect is not always evident. There are layers upon layers of internal inquiry to do before finding our way to the moment in which a last cut lines up our internal and external worlds. This clarity is found through a process of questioning. Feeling like a stranger in one's own life can be painfully uncomfortable. In my experience, the action of a last cut comes with greater ease when clear connection is established to the "why." The "why" presents itself when we ask ourselves powerful questions: What matters most to me? Am I living it? How could I embody and live my values on a more regular basis? What are my choices? What can I let go of, or what do I need more of, in order to establish a life that feels like my own? When we find those answers, we have a framework within which we are able to contemplate action and change. It is a process. Even when we know we are disconnected from our lives and are moved to evaluate what we believe in most, we can be met with resistance and fear. Who do you think you are to want more? In exploring our choices for a different way, we confront our worthiness and our belief systems around standing up for ourselves. The questioning phase builds on itself. The clarity found here feeds into all our last cuts and our evolving sense of self.

"What is most true is the desire to never stop discovering and, for me, the discovery is limitless. Discovery of myself. Discovery of others. Discovery of what the world has to offer. This inner voice inside of me is always giving me advice and direction on where should I go, where should I not go. I think that is what is most true. I love it and I am learning to really allow myself the space to take a full look—a 360-degree look—at what that journey is."

—RONNY TURIAF
Former professional basketball player and current
NBA ambassador

"Honesty is what drives me, but in order to be honest, you have to understand who you are."

—VANESSA CUCCIA

Ask the questions. Take responsibility for the answers.

1.26.17

What is most true to me?

How am I living it?

Where might I still not be living those values?

What action can I take to remedy that disconnect?

11.22.16

How do I show up in the world?

Am I taking the time to quiet the noise and gain clarity?

Am I dreaming big enough?

11.22.16

How do I live my values and uphold my truths while softening my heart and fostering beauty?

How do I hold my vision and a loved one's hand?

How do I remain captivated by my work and drive and allow myself to simultaneously be captivating?

5.4.17

What does freedom mean to me?

11.22.16

What am I willing to let go of to feel whole?

What is weighing me down?

What do I need to toss out to feel more like myself?

9.29.16

What have I ignored?

What have I tolerated?

Where do I need greater voice and clarity to be an agent of change for myself and others?

3.8.18

What (who) defines my identity?

Who am I and how do I want to feel?

3.2.17

What if the very thing I am holding on to is actually that which I most need to release?

11.30.17

What parts of myself do I consistently critique?

Have I ever stopped to wonder why?

Is the distaste my own, or have I internalized a societal norm or belief?

Perhaps if I follow the questioning to the true source, I will see that what I am rejecting is actually what I find most beautiful about myself.

5.16.17

What do I need to let go of to open to greater freedom?

What do I need to own to allow deeper beauty?

What do I need to change to create more peace?

11.16.16

How can I commit more deeply to who I am and what is most
true to me with ease and grace?

How can I be of greater service without compromising my
own well-being?

How can I reach beyond what I know is possible while staying
grounded in myself in the process?

11.18.16

What needs to fall away or be added so I can live a life that feels like my own?

I can attempt to fight what is and what I know to be right (within and around me), but that front only lasts so long. The more I listen and the more I willingly stay open to change, the sooner I end up exactly where I am meant to be.

8.20.17

Do I stay in the brokenness, or do I search deep within to ask the questions that pave the way for lasting transformation?

Do I ask why others have betrayed me or focus on how I have betrayed myself?

Do I care about other people's ignorance and apathy or focus on the places that perhaps I can be less ignorant and apathetic?

11.9.16

Asking the questions leads me to where I want to go and who I want to be. How I get there always becomes clear in the process. Evolution happens one truthful answer at a time.

5.17.17

I trust the truth that lives within me. I have (am) the answer.

1.25.18

If something does not feel right, it is my responsibility to continue to ask the questions in order to identify the root of the disharmony and decay. And when I identify something that is off, I have the power to decide whether to make a last cut.

7.28.16

"I love the man that can smile in trouble, that can gather strength from distress, and grow brave by reflection. 'Tis the business of little minds to shrink; but he whose heart is firm, and whose conscience approves his conduct, will pursue his principles unto death."

—THOMAS PAINE

I desire to be seen and held by a love more vulnerable, raw, and deep than I've ever known before. The road to those moments begins with my willingness to soften and open and create space for the very thing I wish to welcome.

5.4.17

I wonder at times how my strength coexists with my desires, how my inner "superhero" walks with my vulnerable humanity, and how my determination and vision live with my longing. How do I uphold the complex nature of who I am without one part dominating or another overwhelming or diminishing? Can I love myself wholly, as I do, and simultaneously desire to be loved by another? Can I be strong and brave and still long to be held? Can I feel more integrated than ever and still wonder through what lens others see this body, this being (intact or broken)? Layered desires and determinations live beneath this scarred chest and pulse through me at once. I am a dynamic being with otherworldly vision and human desires.

10.4.17

Shame, guilt, and fear paralyze. Vulnerability, truth, education, action, integrity, and humility mobilize.

11.9.16

A missed opportunity is an invitation to do better or different next time.

4.20.17

the (perpetual) motion of the pursuit of my (ongoing) evolution

6.2.17

who do you think you
are to want more?

"I finally felt like I was starting to assess my choices and make the one that was right for me. You know? So when I consumed my whole chest with a chest tattoo and found a tattoo artist who was willing to do it, that was an extremely liberating moment for me—when I stopped listening to what other people wanted me to do and I started doing what I wanted. That was my transition into this newfound power that I didn't know I had before."

—DANA DONOFREE
founder of AnaOno Intimates

When used wisely, my "yes" is one of the most powerful tools for generating happiness, wellness, and freedom.

When used wisely, my "no" is one of the most powerful tools for generating happiness, wellness, and freedom.

11.5.16

I have no idea of the profound capacity for change within or around me until I face that which I run from and prefer to deny or ignore. Truth is not always pretty, but it is surely an agent for change and eventually paves the way to freedom.

2.5.17

I choose...

Commitment

There is no telling how long the questioning phase may last, but we eventually arrive in a moment of inner knowing that is felt within our body. A landing. A grounding. A knowing. Sometimes that clarity is a decision to keep things as they are. Sometimes we know we must let go of something, someone, or a belief, and other times we know we must commit to taking on something more. Last cuts can be the addition or subtraction of a thing, a belief, an attachment, a relationship, a career, a calling, or a way of being. A last cut can be a walking away from or a stepping toward. These moments of significant decision at times call for external action and communication, or ask for a commitment to self, be it in writing or belief. We make these choices all the time throughout our days, but take note of the more significant ones that require deep reflection before action.

These moments offer both promise and opportunity, while challenging all we know and all that makes us feel secure. Last cuts carry the added weight of the collateral damage and pain our individual decisions can cause. In stepping into any last cut moment, we declare within and, at times, out into the world, "I am choosing . . ." And with that commitment, we leap into the unknown, trusting that whatever is next will be better than what was. It is often in that moment of pronouncement, of choosing, of believing, that the internal and external voices, the naysayers and the critics, raise the volume. In our movement forward, our own fear and anxiety, or the opinions of others and/ or society, can amplify their messages in an effort to hold us back or dissuade us. Ultimately, making a last cut requires courage and steadfastness on top of clear commitment in order to ensure action.

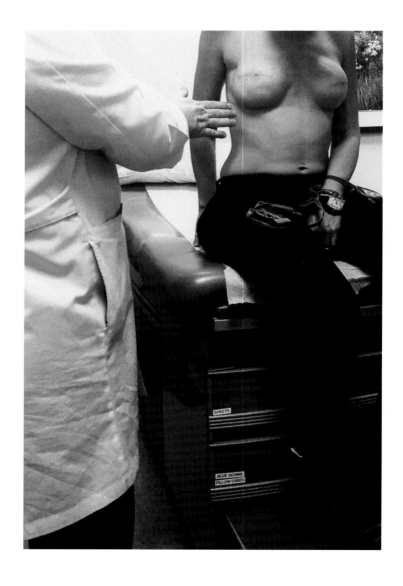

"We get a choice. What do we want to do with it?"

—RONNY TURIAF

"We all get to choose what makes us feel good about ourselves."

—DANA DONOFREE

Last cuts involve a deeply personal and honest assessment of what is happening inside of me in relation to what is happening around me. In those moments of curiosity, desire, disharmony, or pain, I have the power to choose action on behalf of what is most burning inside me. By asking myself questions about my beliefs and reflecting upon how and where to take action, I step into the change for which I yearn. To the best of my ability and within the parameters of extraneous circumstances, I make my internal world begin to match my external one.

A last cut is a significant life decision made to bring one closer to living truth and feeling freer and more fully self-expressed. Last cuts require conscious, healthy, and courageous editing in life. These are the moments when I feel the discomfort of what is not working, what hurts or makes me unwell, and actively choose a different way.

Last cuts do not allow the imposition of others' assumptions or beliefs on my own choices.

Last cuts reject the self-defeating voice in my head that seeks to censor who I truly am.

Last cuts call for learning from the pain, discomfort, messes, and hurt and being brave enough to do it differently the next time. Last cuts ask me to view my life with my own voice and truth as the lens. These difficult, yet powerful, decisions require choosing a sensed freedom and trusting that releasing what does not fit will lead to more space for what does.

3.12.16

We humans falsely believe in the concept of stagnation. Yet there is no stagnation—no such thing as "stuck." There is only movement. There is constant, perpetual motion. Remember, though, that stillness can coexist with all this movement within and around us.

2.1.18

"I've been a prisoner in my own body and chose to break free and did it. And, you know, it's brought me a lot of happiness and a lot of opportunities too. I didn't tell myself I couldn't do this or I couldn't do that. I told myself, 'I will do it.' And I did."

—SERGEANT CHARLIE LINVILLE
The first combat-wounded veteran to climb Mt. Everest

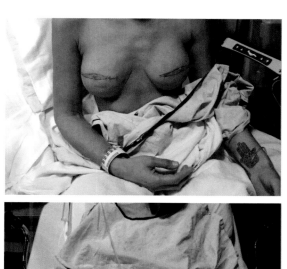

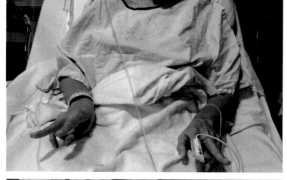

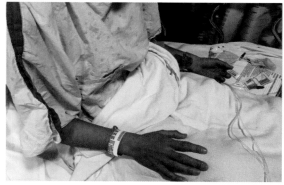

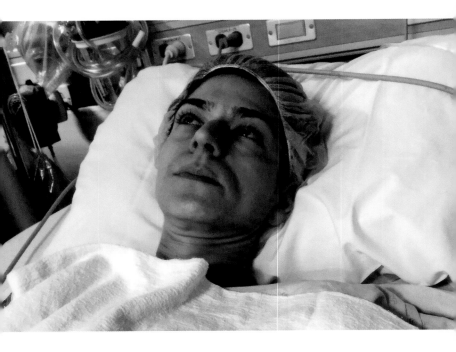

Everything is more challenging when it is forced. When I am clear and
the timing is right, I am choosing to believe that the sky is the limit.

11.28.17

"I feel as if I have come to a massive tipping point, where the sacrifice of letting go of the things that do not meet me in the field of truth is becoming easier and easier, because I am so deeply devoted to staying here in this field."

—ANNE VAN DE WATER
Creator of True Self Mastery

"I spent months in hesitation over decisions that ended up being the best things that could have ever happened to me. It would have happened sooner had I just trusted myself. So I would tell [myself], 'Your crazy dreams are perfectly reasonable.'"

—MONIQUE MITCHELL

"I feel most connected when I'm just holding on to who I am and my truth, doing what I feel is right and pursuing the things that I love, and not worrying about what other people think."

—ANNIE HAWKINS
Professional soccer player

"Freedom, to me, is trusting your own voice, instead of the 'shoulds,' and accepting the messiness that comes along with all of it."

—LILY MANDELBAUM
Cofounder of StyleLikeU

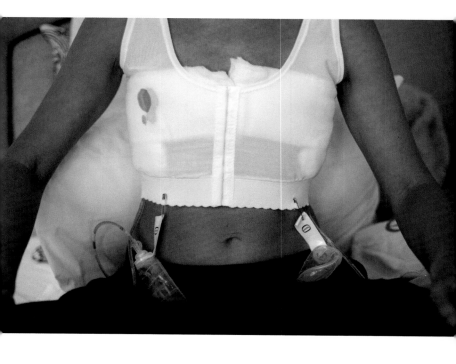

Once I choose a path of self-reflection, I am forever coming back to myself. Every single day. Like all elements in nature, we humans are constantly shedding and evolving, growing and shifting. How I roll with the change is the trick. With more openness and less resistance, I allow the possibility of a deeper inner peace.

6.16.17

I will stand up for what I believe in. I will do all I can to push change. I will keep believing and seeing the good in the world.

11.25.16

While an outcome can never be predicted, my clear choices can point me in the right direction.

9.26.17

Every moment is an opportunity to begin anew. It is easy to carry forth my painful history and project old stories onto every present and future encounter, situation, or circumstance. I have fallen prey to carrying forth the old when it should be left to wither in the past.

9.20.17

No matter where I go, the magical world I create within is always my favorite destination.

7.5.17

Openings. Closings.
Beginnings. Endings.
Nostalgia. Anticipation.
Addition. Subtraction.
Holding. Releasing.
Reflection. Vision.
Arrivals. Departures.

6.10.17

hey, voice, shut up and
let me do my thing

If I take the time to become clear in the quiet, away from the voices,
I know the way to go.

4.25.17

What would I do for myself if I let go of living by what other people think?

2.13.17

We all have voices, both in our heads and around us, that derail us. I have learned over the years to dance with these voices with varying degrees of success. I have found my way by remembering who I am. I have found my way by trusting what is true in my body. Some days, the naysaying voices scream, and others, the voices are kind and encouraging. I can be paralyzed by the voices.

"I should have."

"I could have."

"I should."

"I could."

"I shouldn't."

"I couldn't."

I circled and circled.

I can be distracted by the details and weight of life, or paralyzed by the voices that distract me from action. Now is not the time to hold back what I have to say because I fear someone might judge the validity of my voice. Now is not the time to allow my own naysaying voices to hold me back. Now is the time to ask myself what I believe in most and how I can stand up for it.

11.22.16

Internal and external voices (comparisons/protocols/expectations) can be damaging and outright debilitating. What if there is no right way of being, doing, saying, thinking, existing? What if I were to trust that the timing is always perfect? What if I were to free myself from the hamster wheel of "shoulds"? What if? And what if I remember that my chosen state is (inner) freedom and that, for me, the road there is always found with the vulnerable truth?

7.11.17

Events occur that change not only my external landscape, but also my inner world. Often it's unclear where such transformation begins. Am I motivated to do things differently because of, or in order to alter, what is happening around me? Do I become who I am meant to be due to or in spite of my environment?

1.26.18

Society and the internal/external voices try to convince me that my personal conviction is less important than an ideal or belief held by many. However, denying what I know to be true can have a devastating cost to my health and well-being.

1.5.16

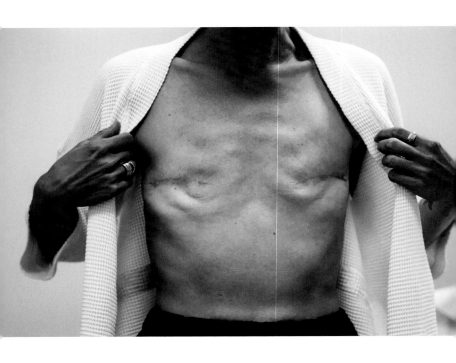

Me: "Do you like it when other people are unkind to you?"
Her: "No."
Me: "Then why is it okay to be unkind to yourself?"
Her: [*thoughtful silence*]

11.16.17

Do I choose strength and wellness in my head, or do I fall prey to the fears and the noise?

3.22.17

"It takes time and energy. It's exhausting and frustrating, because you want to be done. Can I just be healed? There is no such place. There is no finish line, because the more healing you do, the more layers you peel back. There's always something underneath to look at."

—MELINDA ALEXANDER

"It is never-ending. It is this incredible dance of destroying and preserving and re-creating and dying and rebirth in every single moment. That is the dance. That is the truth."

—ANNE VAN DE WATER

"Healing is a matter of time, but it is sometimes a matter of opportunity."

—HIPPOCRATES

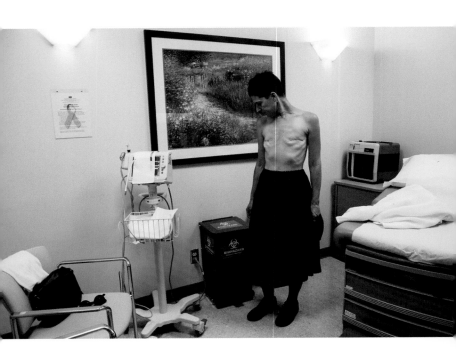

There is no one last cut in any of our lives. Every "last" cut is a desire that this single action will set us free. Yet, we live in a dynamic world. Everything within and around us is constantly evolving. We have a choice as to whether we dedicate ourselves to staying on the pulse of that change so that, to the best of our abilities and circumstances, we are matching up our values with our actions. No one day, no one action, is last and final. True freedom and growth occur when we commit to this philosophy as a way of being.

1.22.17

How do I support myself?

Connection

Last cuts come forth from a deep place within each of us. A disconnect is sensed and questioned. Contemplating choices and action, we can speak to our closest confidants, work colleagues, family members, or even a professional, but in the end, lasting, powerful decisions are sourced within ourselves. Often, we must make last cuts on our own, but we do not have to make them alone. These brave acts are made easier through community and support. There is great value in finding your team—the people in life who have your back and will remind you of the "why," as you navigate life after making a last cut. Who supports me? What nourishes me? How can I take care of myself through this last cut? When we ask ourselves these questions and consider frankly the answers, we prepare for the aftermath of a last cut. We connect with others and ourselves. We take care of ourselves in the midst of change.

Who supports your last cuts?

"One of the most beautiful qualities of true friendship is to understand and to be understood."

—SENECA

"What I (we) need to hear from others is 'I'm here. I'm with you.'"

—JENNIFER YASHARI
Psychiatrist

Samantha Paige and Melinda Alexander

Samantha Paige and Alejandro Ameijeiras

Love fills me up. It feeds me and gives me the strength to
keep showing up, opening up, doing, and giving.

9.10.17

"When I say my poem, I tap into that feeling and I'm just like, okay, I'm going to take all this pain and turn it into empowerment, turn it into real feelings, because I know there's someone out there who has been through everything I've been through and they need someone to tell them they're not alone. Someone to tell them 'I am here for you.'"

—VANESSA TAHAY
Award-winning poet

Through the power of vulnerable conversation and truth telling, I connect with those who inspire and support me in being the best version of myself. By showing up fully in my own life, whatever that means on any given day, I attract the people who truly desire to see me shine in my brilliant individuality.

7.25.17

"The world is so empty if one thinks only of mountains, rivers & cities; but to know someone who thinks & feels with us, & who, though distant, is close to us in spirit, this makes the earth for us an inhabited garden."

—JOHANN WOLFGANG VON GOETHE

Samantha Paige and Jennifer Yashari

Samantha Paige and Ronny Turiaf

Samantha Paige and her daughter

How am I seeing myself and others? Am I looking not only for the strengths, but also for the vulnerabilities and sensibilities?

How am I supporting myself and others, not only in doing, but also in feeling?

7.13.16

Who gets me?

4.12.16

Samantha Paige and her daughter

You ask, "What am I going to do with you?"
I wonder, "What would I do without you?"

2.23.17

"It brings me such emotion to know that people are willing to listen to me. People are willing to feel what I'm feeling and connect."

—VANESSA TAHAY

Silence and an engaged ear are powerful tools for creating connection and for enacting change, especially when my nerves are strained and/or I feel helpless. The act of consciously stopping myself from cutting off another before hearing them out and asking for the same respect in return goes a long way toward fostering dialogue, progress, and peace within, at home and around me.

8.18.17

The power of the pause, of waiting for another to finish a thought,
and to offer response only when it is requested.

8.18.17

"I think, for me, it's connecting internally. That is where the power of meditation and self-reflection comes in, because when you're anchored in feeling a deeper connection to Spirit or who you really are, then what happens externally isn't as dramatic."

—MALLIKA CHOPRA
Author of *Just Breathe: Meditation, Mindfulness, Movement and More*

"The more that I love myself and the more that I take care of myself, the more courage it gives me to let go of the things that don't match."

—ANNE VAN DE WATER

"Stay grounded in yourself." Words I hear. Words I know. Words I tell. The process of learning and embodying this guiding principle, though, takes on a life of its own in the face of what happens around (within) me.

2.22.18

What nourishes me?

What grows in the silence is mighty if I listen.

11.20.17

Because even in the midst of the best of times, I must remember to take care of myself.

Solid nutrition. Slow, deep breathing. Meditation. Alone time. Positive friends. Laughter. Movement. What are the things that keep me going (and sane) in the up, down, and in-between moments?

6.17.17

There are no doubt places that connect me to a greater sense of self. There are places that make me feel at home and at ease. There are places that seem to offer a deepened sense of freedom and space. How, though, do I create home within? How do I create this state of being wherever I am and in the midst of whatever (madness) may be happening around or within me?

2.19.18

I cannot always control what's happening around me. I can do my very best to redirect my thoughts and connect to the landscapes that transport me to a place of peace, regardless of what's happening around me.

12.8.17

Connected disconnect: the art of mindfully checking out to preserve one's sanity, creativity, wellness, and ability to interact with others with grace and calm.

9.12.17

"Let food be thy medicine and medicine be thy food."

—HIPPOCRATES

The truth lives in the body, and every day I have an opportunity to support that truth within myself.

4.12.17

Being in it is beautiful..

Trust

No last cut moment, be it a walking toward something right or away from something wrong, happens overnight. These significant life decisions require courage and clarity, and those come in time and with a commitment to staying with the parts of ourselves from which running would be easier. And even when we finally garner sufficient boldness to walk through the fire and make a last cut, only time knows how long it will take to fully settle into a new state of being. Even when these last cuts are profound moments of arrival, clarity, and knowing, they still call for a period of transition and integration. Because beyond the stories of betrayal, bodily pain, illness, and emotional hurt, how we sit with our most intimate darkness determines our openness to the light.

Would the world (or would we) doubt our decisiveness if we outwardly shared the less than positive and optimistic along the way? The acknowledgment of the full spectrum of our emotions is what makes us human and what helps us heal. Complete willingness to sit in the darkness, sadness, disappointment, anxiety, fear, or pain by no means diminishes the bright victory of the stepping away from or moving toward a new state of being. This process helps us emerge with greater clarity, presence, and willingness to be seen.

These last cut moments can be wholly right and clear, yet still bittersweet. There is sacrifice in growth. There is the need for time to let go of that which was good or that which was holding us back. Every last cut moment—and this happens all the time in varying degrees—is not without a mourning of that which was good and right. Those memories, tears, and markings remind us of what was true in another moment in time. We step out and into new iterations of self that are more fully embodied and exuding what we believe in most, while trusting that the disruptive waters of change are part of the process. Being in it is beautiful.

1.11.17

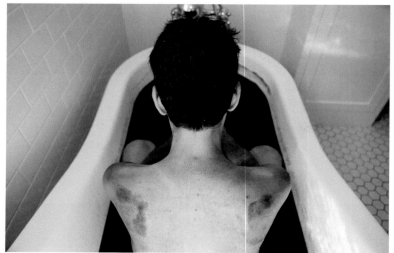

There is often an (internal/external) expectation that I must immediately rebound from a last cut. I have held the belief that, in the wake of any significant decision, I should bounce back and continue on my growth trajectory as if nothing has happened. I fear failure if I cannot weather change without quick progression. Yet, I cannot always see growth under the surface. With time, space, patience, and some nurturing, sweet growth unfolds.

6.12.17

Being in it is beautiful.

3.17.16

And there will too be days,
sometimes weeks,
when there is nothing to do,
but stay with the shadow,
sink deeper into the murky waters,
rest in the darkness,
feel through to the end,
even when the cradle goes cold,
trusting that the learning,
softening,
heartening,
opening,
new beginning,
freedom,
are all just on the other side,
of this chill.

10.27.17

Patience requires trust.
Trust requires patience.
And so it goes.

2.26.18

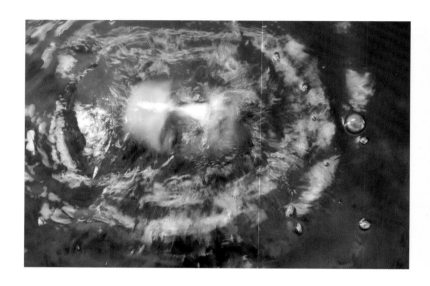

In isolation, integration.

6.27.17

To survive certain experiences in life, I turn to specific parts of myself that are needed in a given moment to see me through to the other side. It is survival. Aspects of self are shut down and others bolstered because it is how I am able to put one foot in front of the other. Compartmentalization allows me to breathe and live another day.

I am faced with the infinite task of integrating who I am in each new moment. With a racing heart and a churning belly, I know that the only way through is to admit my deep desire for softness, vulnerability, and connection and to trust that I will not drown in the admission, but be met and held here as I again rebalance my whole being.

7.8.17

And even when it was challenging, I stayed. In the presence
of the details, both beautiful and disgusting, I recalled the
ever-present capability of seeing myself through anything.

4.6.17

"'There' does not exist. It's right here. That is the profound
shift that needs to happen."

—SASHA MARKOVA
Creative director and writer

"My heart. I've always been fortunate enough to follow my heart, and I consider myself lucky because of that. I've always had support along the way to maybe do what I didn't necessarily think was right or wrong but was what my heart told me to do. Any time I have denied access to that part of my being, it has ended up wrong, so now I've just learned to trust it and go with it."

—DANA DONOFREE

"If we were given the time to just sit and feel wrecked for a while, how significant would that be? We would be so much better off … if we could do it."

—VONN JENSEN
Founder of Flattopper Pride and Queer Cancer

"I'll take sadness—really being with that deep inner child and that buried sadness and all these other things we're covering up—any day over the cover-up. It actually feels good. I'd really like to broadcast that message. It feels so much better to be in the original feeling than to be in the cover-up. The cover-up is far more painful."

—ELISA GOODKIND
Cofounder of StyleLikeU

I lean into something deeper. I trust in the wise messages felt within and let my body do its thing.

6.7.17

Through my commitment to finding light amid darkness within, I strengthen and prepare myself to go out into the world as a force of change.

My darkness can be its own breathing being. It umbrellas the parts within that remind me of pain, shame, heartache, struggle, and vulnerability and houses the parts within that I am told by society are better left aside. I am made to believe there is more value in the light. Yet, I do not have one without the other. I experience brighter light as I move forth from the shadowy darkness. The contrast between the two highlights the inherent beauty in the subtlety of being human and my willingness to be with and, more fundamentally, speak of the dark as a bridge to brighter freedom.

12.21.16

The times when I have gotten caught up in the momentum—so many yeses to keep up with what I know I want to create—but at what cost? If the building undermines the well-being, is it forward movement at all?

3.7.18

Because during moments of darkness, I reach for that which brings me most light.

12.10.17

The utter magic of the space in between.

8.3.17

I am learning (again) what it means to be in this human form. I am contemplating where the human meets the spiritual and how they coexist so both have equal playing time. In quieting the distracting and deterring voices within and beyond, I have again strengthened my connection to the knowledge deep within me. My body is still rebuilding and recalibrating, but is it ever not doing so? Through all this, I have trusted with renewed clarity and resolve. And as I continue to restore, I firmly hold on to the guiding "why."

12.2.17

Somewhere amid the urge to do (force/control/fight/go/create/love), there is patience.

3.29.17

"I want to surrender!" I cried to the wind.
"Then surrender," the wind replied.
"I'm working on it," I called back.

11.21.17

I have been faced with the undeniable truth felt in the body, and as I sift through the answers, words are catching up with the physical and psycho-emotional sensations in the wake of truths spoken, decisions made, and desires expressed.

6.6.17

Photo by Jacopo de Bertoldi

Unraveling the infinite layers of being seen.

5.2.17

LAST CUT

I speak of a truth living in the body and of the messages this body shares with me. I feel at peace when mind and body are in sync. For the last three weeks, my body has had a mind of its own. I feel as if I am moving through molasses. Every cell seems twisted and turned inside out. I continue to do what I know to do: eating the right foods for my body, exercising even as I hold back tears, trying to sleep plenty, and trusting that this is just a phase. I am recognizing how once I turned the corner for the better with my health, I have secretly dreaded being back in a pocket like this one. Old illness-induced trauma cries, "What if I get stuck here again?" I have become accustomed to a healthy, vibrant well-being as my norm. My heart is swelling with compassion for the years (more than a decade) I lived my life feeling like a stranger in this body and for the many who know that existence far too well. I am doing my best not to judge this moment as some failure on my part. My mind desires to understand the "why" behind the feeling and to entice me to try a little bit harder. Perhaps there is no "why." Perhaps it is not about trying harder, but about resisting less. Perhaps it is about total surrender to this and every other phase, both past and present.

11.3.17

As defined in the Merriam-Webster dictionary, "resilience" is "1) the capability of a strained body to recover its size and shape after deformation caused especially by compressive stress; 2) an ability to recover from or adjust easily to misfortune or change." Change, be it in body, mind, environment, or circumstance, happens whether sought after or not, and even when we desire change, we navigate the (sometimes bumpy) road to a new equilibrium. So the question then becomes: How can I meet the shifting tides with openness and resilience?

8.1.17

LAST CUT

Crisis makes me get clear on what truly matters, but how do I carry that forth with intention, grace, and calm?

12.23.17

"I am safe.
I am strong.
I am stable.
I am supported,"
I said to myself in a dream, or was I awake?

3.3.18

"I love you and I am doing my best." Some days those are the only words to say to myself and those around me. And with a long exhale, I keep showing up, doing my best, and loving as big and hard as I know how.

8.15.17

A last act brings more...

Embodiment

To seek to fill and be filled externally is far easier than taking the time to figure out how to be present, to be available, and to care for ourselves. The ongoing effort is far worth the pause, pondering, and pain that accompany a firm dedication to self-discovery. The possibility of love for self, and others, beyond each last cut grows deeper than we can imagine.

Embodiment of self does not happen overnight. Embodiment of self requires commitment, compassion, and forgiveness. Embodiment of self requires a willingness to sit with, work with, pull apart, and eventually own the parts within and without that make up who we are. Following a last cut, we can awaken and open to the newness. We hope to arrive and embody the change we have embraced. In time, we seek to experience a version of ourselves that we could have only imagined and feel at home in our skin.

3.28.16

A last cut brings more openings.

A last cut brings more lightness.

A last cut brings more illumination.

A last cut brings more solidity.

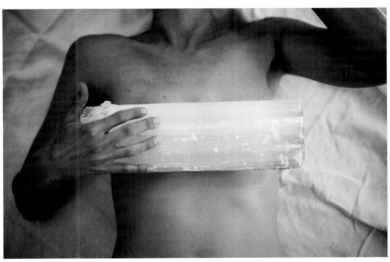

A last cut brings more magic.

When launched from clarity, vision, and trust, we find connected
beauty and openings.

Through the love of self, an awakening to love.

In the knowing, an opening.

5.2.17

Stronger love has grown in my life since I committed to loving myself. Relationships have become more nourishing, powerful, and special. Old connections have deepened. New ones (the healthy new ones) arrive there more quickly. In looking back, I have compassion for the young(er) woman who sought to love and be loved without a firm grounding within herself yet. The person who said yes to being, thinking, acting, and looking a certain way with the hope of being loved for doing the right thing and of fitting into an acceptable mold.

2.14.18

The road to embodiment is not always direct.

11.16.16

This vehicle consistently breathes, processes, digests, makes, removes, moves, builds, breaks down, swallows, chews, and holds me. I used to mistrust it. I flat-out feared it. At some point along the way, instead of tearing it apart, I made the choice to hold it up, to trust it, to make friends with it, to see it and honor it. It is mine. It is unique. It is beautiful.

5.16.17

Every scar on this body marks a time in my life
when I have experienced pain, growth, and
unbelievable healing. It's trying at times, but it's
magical to be in this body.

10.19.17

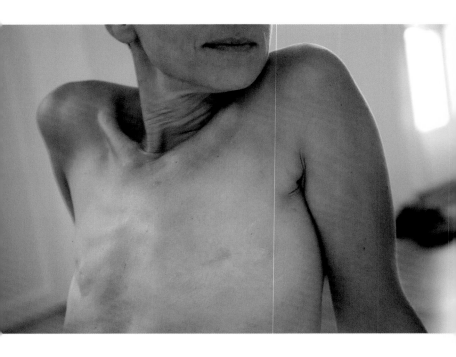

My nine-year-old daughter said, "Mama, this is amazing, because you get to show other women what it feels like to love being in your body." Every day I think about how each action I make communicates to my daughter.

3.2.17

"Normal" is a dangerous word. I have been taught to ingest some version of normal to which I am expected to conform. Being the same may be more comfortable for others, but in reality we are all unique and different. Normal is not a box to check. Normal is what makes each of us feel at home in our own body. I finally found the strength to live by what feels best for me, because I know how awful it can be to feel like a stranger in your own life. I did it for years and felt disconnected and numb. So embracing my uniqueness was a lifeline.

10.10.17

My scars were harbingers of the opportunity to take
care of and love myself more deeply.

5.16.17

"But you're perfect," she said.
"According to whom?" I replied in surprise, as I lifted
up my shirt to reveal my cut up chest.
"You're just perfect," she said again.
"Only because I think I am. You are perfect too. You
just need to believe it," I offered back.

11.18.17

I claim and own every scar. I cured and healed.
I overcame pain. I birthed a human. I stood up for
myself. I voiced. I severed, cut, and added. Perhaps my
beauty may not always be conventional, or what I see
in magazines and movies, but it is mine.

6.13.17

Why do I feel the need to hide the normal bits and spots that we all have, at one time or another? Why do I withhold aspects of myself or only see where I am lacking (or gaining)? The more I have shared and owned the parts of myself that previously evoked shame, embarrassment, or fear, the more I have found peace, happiness, and deeper connection with self and others.

5.22.17

"You are what you can mentally achieve, not what you perceive your body capable of."

—CHARLIE LINVILLE

"Everything that makes you different or weird, or that you have struggles [with], or that makes you feel insecure next to the next person, is what makes you awesome. If everyone could just accept their unique makeup and all the different qualities that they possess, then that would be a beautiful thing."

—LILY MANDELBAUM

The body knows the truth. When I listen to its signals,
I open myself up to beauty never imagined.

4.25.17

We are full-spectrum human beings. The more familiar
I become with the pain and darkness, the broader
bandwidth for love and connection I too experience.

12.29.17

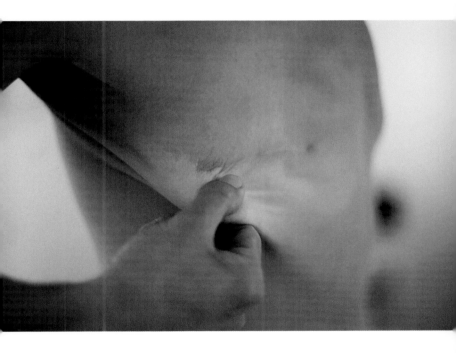

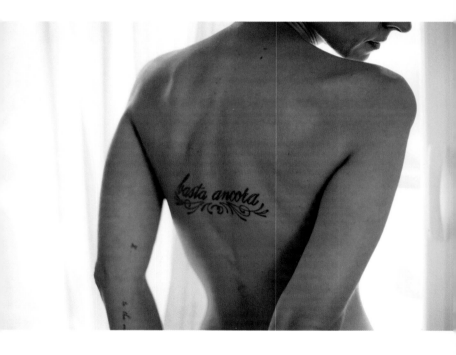

Reclamation of innocence.

10.25.17

the whisper of your voice
the trail of a hand
traces the lines across my chest
abdomen
heart
parallels meet perpendiculars
drawn and crossed
hardened and softened
opened and closed
markings become maps
sewn so tightly shut
now opened
gaping
raw
rising
falling
breathing
lines
drawn
cut
created
symbol above word
open roads
straight
to
my
pulse

—"openings"

7.23.17

Honoring the moments (days) that wake me up to who I am and what I believe in most.

10.8.17

A beautiful merging of past and present iterations of self.

Loving compassion for every version of self.

4.18.17

I rest into my uniqueness and emanate my beauty always.

3.12.17

Embodied freedom: the feeling obtained when one's inner landscape matches the life one creates and lives out in the world; also see "presence," "congruency," and "truth."

9.16.17

For the first time in my memory, I feel whole and well.

7.28.16

I heard, "I welcome the light," and
I stepped into the day wondering
what phrase would be next.

8.27.17

freedom =

Freedom

Last cuts are the brave decisions that bring congruency to our values and actions, thereby allowing for greater freedom. Freedom comes when we identify, honor, and live by our personal truth. We ask the questions, commit to the truth, and take action to line up who we are on the inside with the life we are living out in the world. When our internal and external worlds are congruent, we feel greater freedom. Lasting freedom starts on the inside and radiates out into the world.

The freedom on the other side of a last cut may take a while to make itself fully known, but when it does, oh, it's sweet.

1.8.17

I will continue to ask the
questions. I will continue to act
on behalf of what I believe in
most, and I will vulnerably and
truthfully talk about it.

11.22.16

Here's to being open to deep self-inquiry and embracing all that shows up, walks away, dies off, morphs, and is reborn. Here's to being willing to dance with the self and stay present in the universe. Death. Rebirth. Repeat.

8.10.17

Freedom = (How do I hold my commitment to freedom and honor my last cuts in new decisions moving forward?)

4.7.16

Never underestimate the power of radical honesty and
change within myself.

10.28.16

The magic. The connection. The words. The believing.
The freedom.

7.4.17

LAST CUT

Intuition is a curious thing. I have found in the moments when my inner knowing (insert whatever word you prefer—intuition, gut feeling, sixth sense, etc.) is the strongest, simultaneously my mind can increase the naysaying, second-guessing chatter. A clear feeling in the body that says yes or no can become completely muddled when the mind says, "If you say yes (or no), you might be missing out on x, y, or z," or "If you say yes (or no), you might be wrong or closing the door to an opportunity," or, better yet, "You should want to do this." What if there were no right or wrong? What if "should" and guilt were tossed aside for good? What if I were to trust that those moments of clarity are exactly that? Clarity. A knowing of self. What if there did not always have to be a rational, intellectual explanation for turning down something that looks great on paper? What if?

Stepping into that space is incredibly liberating.

8.4.17

Unbridled joy. The happiness I feel when I do not filter, when I forget my trauma, when I am fully and wholly present. Having once again tapped into this sensation of glee and wild abandon multiple times recently, I am desiring more of it, because I know what it fills me with and how the thoughts that no longer serve me melt away so gracefully in its presence.

8.24.17

Acceptance of, gratitude for, and peace with all the chapters and choices that led to this moment.

4.18.17

Reflect.

Release.

Regroup.

Resist.

Relate.

Reach.

Release.

Reclaim.

Revisit.

Represent.

Relish.

Relax.

Rejoice.

Release.

Radiate.

Repeat.

—"living my life"

8.29.16

First and last replaced by most recent. The power of the past diminished
by the present. The hypothetical what-if quietly sitting with the
stripped-down beauty of what is.

12.30.17

I spend so much time envisioning, dreaming, and planning. I work diligently to succeed and to claim. I strive and set forth, imagining an arrival, grasping for a dream, or willing a departure. One chapter ends and another begins, sometimes unrecognizably and often distinctly. Yet as I leap into the new, the memory of the old whispers distantly from where I came. I find myself suspended in the space between departure and arrival, at the intersection of launch and landing. I am no longer yearning for a distant point on the map, but recognize I am standing where I had longed to be. And from this place, I can see where I have been as clearly as the coordinates of my next destination. I am at once here and there, and far beyond.

1.15.17

Open Space

4.5.16

"Freedom, to me, is choice."

—ZOË BUCKMAN
Multidisciplinary artist

"Freedom, for me, has been having freedom from self-criticism and all of the kinds of internal mandates and goals that you set for yourself."

—MALLIKA CHOPRA

"Freedom means that you don't have to earn something to be worth something."

—ANNIE HAWKINS

"Freedom, to me, is where you live a happy, unpersecuted life, free to do whatever you want and not be judged."

—CHARLIE LINVILLE

"Freedom overall is the concept of normal being a distant memory, and nobody feels pressured to conform, or nobody gets policed, or nobody gets attacked for not fitting that strict definition of normal."

—PIDGEON PAGONIS
Intersex activist, educator, and filmmaker

"I know now that love is energy, and I know that we are love so we are energy. And I understand that when we are on a higher vibration and we are true to ourselves and we speak, act, and live from a love standpoint, we are at the highest vibration we can be. We all know what that feels like. It feels like bliss and it feels like joy and it feels like laughter."

—JOSETTE TKACIK
Zumba instructor and medical miracle

"Freedom, to me, is being able to fail. Accept your failures. Accept the parts of yourself that you don't love or like. To be wrong and be okay with it. To not be governed by your ghosts and your past—to be able to let it go and be present."

—ELISA GOODKIND

"When you have the truth, it's really freedom, because what you decide to do or what you talk about, everything comes from the truth. That's what freedom is about."

—SOFIA LINDVALL
Stuntperson and nature lover of Treehotel in Harads, Sweden

Beyond me ...

Epilogue

I write the story to right the story.
5.30.17

Sharing one's most intimate thoughts and feelings is somewhat akin to throwing oneself off a cliff without guarantee of a safe landing. There is no way to predict how our expressions of vulnerability and truth will be received. A desire for freedom beyond shame, secrecy, and hurt leads us to the edge, a place where words meet feeling. We find ourselves with little choice but to set them loose to fly off into the world. These openings do not always look one way; expression can happen in myriad forms, be it writing in a journal, having a conversation with a loved one, or, as is so often the case these days, posting on social media.

The reason I share has little to do with anticipated reception. I do it for survival. I learned the hard way over the years that my wellness requires that I give voice to the full spectrum of feelings that coexist within me. I must relieve the pressure that can build within myself in order to stay well and, quite frankly, sane. I have experienced time and time again that pain left untouched causes more hurt. What festers within us can make us sick in one manner or another. For years, I explored a controlled "pretend as if everything is okay" way of being and found myself isolated, lost, and tempered by prescription medications to handle the anxiety and depression that welled up within me around the untold hurt.

In the decision to share about my explant surgery through *Last Cut Project* back in January 2016, there was indeed a desire for relief and a hope for connection. Perhaps if I threw my story out there into the world in a fairly public way, there might be one other person who would raise their hand and say, "Yes. I know this pain too." I was curious what might transpire if I chose to communicate this particular last cut, and in doing so the ones preceding and following, and so I began writing of my decision to remove my implants. I have since been deeply moved by the dialogue started and the community built. My words of truth and the raw, intimate images captured by photographer Lisa Field fostered a conversation that continues to grow far beyond my personal story. My experience acted as a magnet for others to join me at the edge of comfort and control. While the details of our stories differ widely, the humanity underneath the surface of each tale connects us all. Through community, we find strength. In time, we hopefully find peace, forgiveness, closure, love, and, of course, freedom. There is incredible liberation in committing to change and profound healing in the telling. The metaphor of the explant, whether that of silicone implants or any other inconsistency we carry within us, will remain fundamental to

Last Cut Project, and my chest scars mark one of the most transitional times of my life.

What has been most astounding throughout this first chapter of *Last Cut Project* have been the ways in which I have met the people and opportunities that naturally— somewhat cosmically—determined the next steps of the journey. Expression has fostered connection. One day in the fall of 2016, I received an email from an agent at an international casting agency who had seen my website, inquiring about my interest in attending a casting for Equinox, an international luxury fitness club brand, for its 2017 Commit to Something campaign. At first I said to Lisa, "This must be a joke." After the initial shock and with Lisa's encouragement, I wrote back expressing interest.

Soon thereafter, I found myself telling my story in front of the creative agents and Equinox team, including Equinox executive creative director Elizabeth Nolan, a casting agent, and a photographer. I shared the details of my decades-long health journey

Samantha Paige and Elena Venetia in Equinox's 2017 Commit to Something campaign.
Photograph by Steven Klein

Samantha Paige in front of Equinox's 2017 Commit to Something billboard on Sunset Boulevard
in West Hollywood, California.

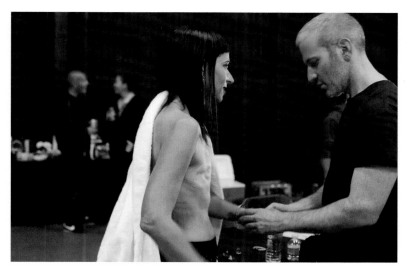

Samantha Paige with stylist Mel Ottenberg on the set for Equinox's 2017
Commit to Something photo shoot on October 8, 2016.

Samantha Paige with hairstylist Chris McMillan on the set for Equinox's 2017 Commit to Something photo shoot on October 8, 2016.

Samantha Paige with hairstylists Chris McMillan and Pete Lamden on the set for Equinox's 2017 Commit to Something photo shoot on October 8, 2016.

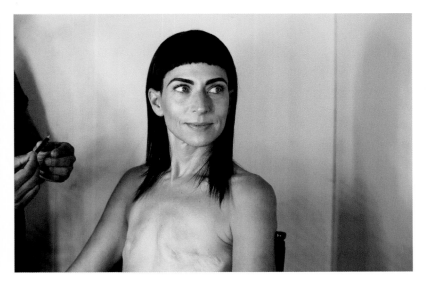

Samantha Paige having her makeup done for Equinox's 2017 Commit to Something photo shoot on October 8, 2016.

and recent decision to explant. After conversing for a half hour or so, one of the creatives asked if I would be willing to take my shirt off to show my flat chest. The modeling job I was auditioning for was to be an image of a topless post-mastectomy woman having a chest tattoo done by a female tattoo artist in a swanky tattoo parlor. Being both excited for the opportunity to be part of the campaign and comfortable in my skin and in front of the camera (especially after working with Lisa on *Last Cut Project*), I did not hesitate before taking off my top. I bared my chest scars and spoke of last cuts and the power of storytelling to heal our wounds and connect us with a supportive community. I spoke of owning my scars and learning to love every iteration of myself. We recorded some video footage and test shots for the campaign's photographer, Steven Klein, who was not present for the audition, but would be part of the creative planning process. When I finished sharing my story, most in the room were in tears. I left the audition feeling as if that experience alone was healing and impactful for me. A week later,

I was offered the job to model for Equinox's campaign.

I could only have dreamt this opportunity would present itself in my lifetime. The chance to be styled by Mel Ottenberg and hair visionary Chris McMillan and to model for Steven Klein was unbelievable. I was over the moon with excitement on a personal level, but beyond that, I was in awe of the opportunity to broaden the platform for *Last Cut Project*. I had shared my story and scars with the *Last Cut Project* community and then was offered a global stage. When the image of me, bare-chested in my power, getting a tattoo, launched in January 2017, the reach of my personal story and mission expanded exponentially around the world. Equinox shared my image on billboards, through print and video campaigns, and on the walls in all its gyms. I am forever grateful for the occasion.

Equally profound have been the friendships I have made through this project. From the incredible individuals I have met through social media, to the changemakers

Samantha Paige and Yuri Angela Chung at SITE 57 Gallery for the *Notes to a Friend*: The Experience and *EXPLANT* exhibitions in October 2017.

I have interviewed for the *Last Cut Conversations* podcast, to the serendipitous encounters with people at speaking events and out in the world, my life is richer for the people with whom I have connected through *Last Cut Project*. This list is long and the relationships, for which I am grateful, many.

The tale of how I found the work of Yuri Angela Chung, who eventually wrote the foreword to this book, on Instagram is a beautiful one. Just weeks after my explant surgery, my dear friend Melissa helped me run a bath and told me that while I soaked I had to read *Notes to a Friend*, written by Yuri, who was diagnosed with breast cancer at age twenty-five and again in her early thirties. Each word shared by Yuri pulled me in closer. She beautifully expressed so much that I had experienced as a young adult cancer patient in my early twenties and as an individual constantly learning over and over again what it is like to be a changing body.

Yuri and I became friends through Instagram. Then via email, Yuri

invited *Last Cut Project* to exhibit a twelve-image show, entitled *EXPLANT*, in conjunction with her *Notes to a Friend* installation in New York City in honor of breast cancer awareness month in October 2017. Even though we lived within a couple of hours of each other in Southern California, it was not until opening night of our gallery show that we first met in person. The perfect opportunities, connections, and relationships always do appear at the right time. This person I may never have met in day-to-day life was now intimately woven into the fabric of my life and heart. I will forever be grateful for the time we had together before Yuri passed away in November 2018.

I am also forever changed by a chance encounter with a Zimbabwean refugee I met in London at the Victoria and Albert Museum at a "Living Library" event held during Refugee Week by the Migration Collective, a group of dynamic and creative women who aim to challenge the current narrow rhetoric on migration through projects at the intersection of art, academia, and action. This woman's parents were killed, perhaps murdered, in Zimbabwe, and she was nearly beaten and tortured to death herself. She eventually landed in London, where she received medical treatment to rebuild her crushed forehead and heal, both physically and emotionally, from the trauma. At the end of our deep chat in the beautiful courtyard of the museum, she said, "Now I want to use my scars and stories to help other people. I tell my stories to heal myself and hopefully to make other people feel less alone." I teared up when she expressed to me words I myself have said thousands of times. She asked about my life, and I shared the highlights of my story. I said, "My story seems trivial in light of yours," as there was so much more to her triumphant story of survival, and my own is laced with privilege and relative ease. She replied, "Trauma is trauma. We all have our own stories."

Samantha Paige in front of Last Cut Project's *EXPLANT* exhibition
at SITE 57 Gallery in October 2017.

Last Cut Project's *EXPLANT* exhibition at SITE 57 Gallery in October 2017.

Samantha Paige and Last Cut Project photographer Lisa Field at the opening for Last Cut Project's *EXPLANT* exhibition at SITE 57 Gallery in October 2017.

I have spent more than just these past few years dedicated to making last cuts and making peace. It has been a long twenty-year journey of physical pain and the emotional fallout that came along with it. I have loved and lost people, places, and parts of my body and ultimately committed myself to finding love and forgiveness within and without. The opportunity to share and process all of this through *Last Cut Project* has clarified my truth, generated a deeper sense of community and connection, and set me free from the pain of feeling like a stranger in my own life. I never thought I would find such clarity. I hope to inspire others to trust that through the asking of the difficult questions of themselves and honoring their truth, freedom is on the other side.

10.8.16

last cut conversations

Last Cut Conversations

Last Cut Conversations is the *Last Cut Project* podcast that launched in 2016. Just months into working on *Last Cut Project* with photographer Lisa Field, it became apparent that the conversation we were documenting around my explant surgery was one we wished to have in concert with more individuals and their significant last cut moments. So I began to reach out to people I know and admire to ask if they were open to talking with me about their last cuts made to create a life that feels more like their own. I was honored by the responses I received and the dialogue that ensued, both in the recordings and through the broader *Last Cut Project* community.

The first season of *Last Cut Conversations* focused on individuals opening up about what they believe in most, how they are living those beliefs, and often a specific last cut that highlights this connection. The second season of *Last Cut Conversations* centered around the idea of freedom, what this concept means to each of us, and how we create it within ourselves and speak up for it outside in the world against systems that seek to homogenize and limit us, collectively and individually. These conversations are always honest and raw. They are also deeply personal and universal.

For this book, I selected quotes and imagery from those interviews that best matched what I desired to outline here regarding the seven universal steps of making a last cut. Even though this book does not include every *Last Cut Conversations* participant, every individual whom I spoke with has profoundly impacted me and this work. It takes a tremendous amount of courage to vocalize one's personal story, beliefs, and vulnerabilities. When we do so, we are able to both honor the particulars of our unique tales and foster community around our shared humanity. I am forever grateful to each person who trusted me and Lisa with their story in words and imagery. I honor each of you and thank you for your bravery and grace.

Melinda Alexander

I had heard of the legendary Melinda Alexander, who is known online as MuMu Mansion, and was thrilled to meet her in person following an introduction through Elle Communications. In 2017, Melinda and I sat down in her studio to speak about love, self-healing, parenting, and the gift of learning from life's most challenging moments. Melinda is an all-around lover, mother, healer, and social activist who does womxn's work in many forms to heal herself and others. She is dedicated to learning from the internal and external conversations about life, while vulnerably and boldly welcoming thousands on her personal journey. Following the birth of her son and a painful divorce, she revolutionized her life and created a broad platform to show the possibilities born with the willingness to learn from what is not working. Melinda proved to herself that she had the power within to get through anything if she stayed open to extracting the information—the evolution—found in even the most difficult moments. Our candid *Last Cut* Conversation touched upon love, healing, parenthood, race, divorce, trauma, the beauty in discomfort, and the power of transforming pain.

For more information on Melinda Alexander's powerful work, please visit melinda-alexander.com and @mumumansion on Instagram. Her powerful book, entitled Getting Free: A Love Story *(a must-read for all who love candor and vulnerability), is available on her website.*

Alejandro Ameijeiras

In the *Last Cut* Conversation we shared, Santa Barbara, California-based Pilates instructor and dancer Alejandro Ameijeiras shares his long, sometimes dark, road to personal acceptance and embodiment of his sexuality, sensitivity and inner power. Born in Communist Cuba to prominent diplomats in 1963, he grew up in a culture that was beautiful in many ways, but far from accepting of individual differences. He studied first as a professional swimmer, then in military school and eventually as a dancer. Being the son of a top general was at times in contrast to who he was and knew he wanted to be. Alejandro left Cuba in his late teens to train with the Bolshoi Ballet in Moscow. He then traveled with the Tropicana troupe in East Germany and Italy right before the Berlin Wall came down. After further exploring his dancing and modeling career in Cuba, he finally left for Panama in 1995 and arrived in Miami on Christmas Eve in 1997. Years, and much dedicated internal work, later, he has created a dream life in California with a loving husband, thriving Pilates business and ever-evolving inner peace, due to his ongoing dedication to personal growth and self-discovery.

Zoë Buckman

Zoë Buckman is a multidisciplinary visual artist, activist, and mother. Originally from East London, she now lives and works in New York City. Zoë weaves together art and activism into powerful pieces that draw viewers in with aesthetically pleasing beauty, while offering an undercurrent that inspires deeper contemplation on political issues. Zoë spoke to the process of transforming what she sees happening in the world around her into thought-provoking works of art. With creations such as *Let Her Rave, Mostly It's Just Uncomfortable*, and *Every Curve*, her work beautifully combines the feminine with the fierce, sparking conversation around feminism, mortality, and equality. In our *Last Cut* Conversation, recorded in New York in October 2017, Zoë shared how her activism informs her art and how both inform her parenting of her young daughter. After admiring Zoë's work for years, I was excited to sit down with her to talk about art, activism, the shared experience of mothering daughters in this moment in time, and the power of last cuts to wake us up and foster change.

To learn more about Zoë Buckman's visual art and upcoming projects, please visit zoebuckman.com or @zoebuckman on Instagram.

Mallika Chopra

Mallika Chopra is a mother, author, speaker, and entrepreneur. Her books include *Living with Intent: My Somewhat Messy Journey to Purpose, Peace, and Joy*; *100 Promises to My Baby*; and *100 Questions from My Child*. She is the founder of IntentBlog.com, an online community where members can share their dreams and aspirations, and receive support from others to do the same. Mallika joined me for a powerful conversation about living life with intent and about conscious parenting. In her humble and authentic manner of sharing, Mallika detailed her self-described "somewhat messy journey" to deeper purpose, peace, and joy in all aspects of life. With anecdotes from her life and conversations with her father, Deepak Chopra, and friend Eckhart Tolle, she modeled how we can set clear intentions to create greater balance in all areas of our lives. She shared her belief that conscious parenting requires mindfulness in speech and actions with our children, as well as a continuous reflection on our deepest desires for the journey as a parent. We discussed how she is raising two empowered, engaged feminists through her family's honest sharing of what is happening in the world and how she is always modeling the need to connect with self in order to navigate everything with grounded confidence.

For more information on Mallika Chopra's work, please visit mallikachopra.com and @mallikachopra on Instagram, Twitter and Facebook. Mallika's latest book, entitled Just Breathe: Meditation, Mindfulness, Movement and More, *was released at the end of August 2018. For kids ages 8 to 12, this is an accessible and fun meditation and mindfulness how-to book filled with full-color illustrations, written by Mallika Chopra and with a foreword by Deepak Chopra.*

Vanessa Cuccia

I had the incredible pleasure of meeting Vanessa Cuccia, founder of Chakrubs, a company that creates sex toys from natural crystal that bring a sense of sacredness to one's playtime. Our *Last Cut* Conversation took place in New York on my birthday in 2015, and the whole experience was a gift. I reached out to Vanessa after following her story and stunning Instagram feed. I love everything she writes about—self-love, healing, and awareness—and her aesthetic is gorgeous. Beyond that and the inarguable intrigue of the beautiful crystal sexual wellness products she creates, I knew I was meant to meet this woman, and I was right. I undoubtedly made a new friend for life that day. I was moved by Vanessa's deep self-awareness, honesty, and vision in life. In a moment in history when our world is evidently going through some serious and intense change and evolution, I cannot help but hope that we will find our way through by first finding peace within ourselves. When I meet people like Vanessa, with an evident and ingrained commitment to introspection, growth, and service, I have greater hope for our planet and for the world in which my daughter will grow. I believe it is possible to maintain a deep connection with the self and those who support us regardless of time, space, and distance. When we are open and present, we find new family with whom we can create support along the way. This happens when we are clear on what matters most within, live it, and find others who are doing the same. Vanessa is living this way. I am grateful to know her and share her story.

For more information on Vanessa Cuccia, please visit @vanessa_cuccia on Instagram. For more information on Chakrubs, please visit chakrubs.com, @chakrubs on Instagram and Twitter, Chakrub Crystals on Facebook, or Chakrubs on YouTube. Vanessa's beautiful book, entitled Crystal Healing & Sacred Pleasure, *is available on the Chakrubs website.*

Dana Donofree

Dana Donofree founded AnaOno, a lingerie, loungewear, and swimwear line made for individuals who have had breast surgeries or live with conditions that cause breast pain or discomfort. A breast cancer survivor herself, she created the company out of her own necessity and desire for sexy, beautiful lingerie. Dana was diagnosed with infiltrative ductal carcinoma, an aggressive form of breast cancer, at age twenty-seven and then had a bilateral mastectomy with implant reconstruction. Her own bras no longer fit, and she was certain there must be better options. After discovering her beautiful and functional bras following my explant surgery, I had the pleasure of becoming friends with Dana from across the country. Finally, in December 2016 in New York City, I had the joy of meeting Dana and AnaOno employee Alison Hinch to discuss life after breast cancer and mastectomies, personal growth, and embodiment after illness and trauma. Dana frankly shared about breast cancer and her last cut, the decision to get a mastectomy tattoo years ago, before it was popular to do so. Her choice was a powerful reclaiming of self after all she had been through at a young age. I love Dana's honesty and honor all she does for this community. She shows her collections at New York Fashion Week in partnership with #CancerLand, a New York City nonprofit dedicated to changing the conversation around the disease.

For more information on Dana Donofree, please visit @daynadono on Instagram.

For more information on her gorgeous AnaOno lingerie, loungewear, and swimwear lines, please visit anaono.com, @anaonointimates on Twitter and Instagram, or AnaOno Intimates on Facebook.

Annie Hawkins

In August 2017, I had the opportunity to do a fireside chat about living life from the heart with my dear friend and professional soccer player Annie Hawkins. Annie opened up about losing her father to pancreatic cancer six years prior and how his passing, and, possibly more profoundly, how he lived the last months of his life, inspired her to deepen her own dedication to a meaningful, service-filled, and connected existence. She shared what soccer has taught her over the years, her unique relationship to time, and how she has opened her heart and schedule to traveling the world to connect, explore, and inspire others to live their fullest lives, while remaining radically true to herself. Having met through and shared some sweet adventures with our mutual dear friend Ronny Turiaf, we also addressed the importance of community and friendship when one is living a life outside the box.

For more information on Annie Hawkins, please visit www.the10influence.com, @anniehawkins on Instagram, and @the10influence on Twitter.

Vonn Jensen

Vonn Jensen is a U.S.-based cancer advocate approaching advocacy through the lens of social justice. They founded the movements Flattopper Pride and Queer Cancer and work specifically with populations often disenfranchised or rendered invisible in the dominant breast cancer narrative. Using a variety of media, they have worked for visibility as a means of combating the marginalization that certain groups, such as the queer community, face during treatment. The week before my explant surgery, I found Vonn's Flattopper Pride feed on Instagram. I felt instant relief, as I saw another person feeling at home in their body with no reconstruction after a double mastectomy. Vonn's willingness to share photos, as well as their dedication to normalizing this body type, provided an incredible amount of encouragement and community as I stepped into this new version of myself. Vonn has been a constant reference point and solid support over these past years. In November 2016, while Lisa and I were on a work trip to Portland, Oregon, we finally met up with Vonn to record a *Last Cut* Conversation about Vonn's story, including their advocacy, the concept of breast cancer as a gendered disease, the universal need for balance and self-care, and their vision for a more inclusive landscape in the breast cancer advocacy world.

Sofia Lindvall

Sofia Lindvall was born and raised in Harads, Sweden (population: approximately 600), just sixty kilometers south of the Arctic Circle. She is a trained stuntperson and the daughter of Kent Lindvall and Britta Jonsson-Lindvall, the founders of Treehotel. Treehotel is a collection of seven unique tree houses, designed by Scandinavia's leading architects, where guests can sleep four to six meters up in the trees and commune with nature in a modern, comfortable manner. In the middle of untouched Swedish forest, I met with Sofia to hear the story behind Treehotel and about the love of nature that inspired her family to create this magical place. Honoring and embracing nature is the key to the whole Treehotel experience; incredibly, no trees were cut during its construction. Sofia shared about growing up in a small town in a time of globalization and urbanization, why she left for a bigger city, and what motivated her to return to Harads after one year. Our *Last Cut* Conversation highlighted the beauty of strong interhuman connections, the importance of living in harmony with our natural environment, and the power of slowing down our pace in life.

For more information on the Lindvall family and Treehotel, please visit treehotel.se.

Charlie Linville

In October 2017, I sat down with my friend Charlie Linville to talk about his life-changing last cuts, overcoming trauma, perseverance, adventure, and inspiration on the other side of pain. In 2011, while serving in Afghanistan, Charlie, a marine sergeant, was injured while attempting to dismantle an improvised explosive device (IED) as an explosive ordnance disposal technician. After fourteen surgeries over eighteen months, his injured foot was not healing. Charlie made the ultimate last cut by proactively deciding to amputate his right leg below the knee. Soon after that decision, he committed to training with the Heroes Project and became the first combat-wounded amputee to climb Mt. Everest in 2016. His first attempt was canceled after an avalanche killed sixteen Sherpas in 2014. His second effort was abandoned when Nepal was devastated by a huge earthquake in 2015. Charlie's strength and humility have inspired me since before we first met on an Equinox video shoot in 2016. My mom, who works out at an Equinox gym, had shared his powerful story with me when I started *Last Cut Conversations*. Her email finished with "His story is pretty amazing." After hearing about Charlie from my mom and reading up on his story, I had the good fortune to meet him in person on an Equinox video shoot. A year after that encounter, we sat down to record for the podcast. Charlie and my *Last Cut* Conversation touched upon the universal importance of sharing our stories and trusting in the power of connection to heal ourselves and others.

Lily Mandelbaum and Elisa Goodkind

In May 2017, I met Lily Mandelbaum and Elisa Goodkind, the creators of StyleLikeU, at the signing for their book, *True Style Is What's Underneath: The Self-Acceptance Revolution*, in Los Angeles. Just weeks later, Lily and Elisa interviewed me for their Dispelling Beauty Myths video series with *Allure* magazine in New York. In our *Last Cut* Conversation, I was excited to switch roles and ask the mother-daughter duo powerful questions about their lives. They touched upon life before StyleLikeU, the last cuts they made to step into this creative endeavor, where they find inspiration for and connection to their work, and how they stayed open and vulnerable to and during this transformative process. These two women shared eloquently about the importance of redefining individuality, the value of staying true to oneself in spite of society's homogenizing messages, and the deep connection all beings share. In the same vulnerable spirit of the intimate docu-style video portraits of StyleLikeU, Lily and Elisa opened up to me about the importance of always going deeper within oneself in order to make a bolder contribution in the world.

To connect with Lily Mandelbaum and Elisa Goodkind and discover more about StyleLikeU, please visit stylelikeu.com, StyleLikeU on YouTube and Facebook, or

@stylelikeu on Instagram and Twitter. Their book, entitled True Style Is What's Underneath: The Self-Acceptance Revolution, *is available through their website and on Amazon.*

Sasha Markova

I met Sasha Markova through our sweet mutual friends. Initially, we shared occasional, yet meaningful conversations at many a birthday party. After weaving in and out of each other's landscapes with little regularity, a few years ago Sasha led me to an oasis in Death Valley and inspired me to let my creative flag fly. I then rented a space in Echo Park from her for a year that offered a creative incubator for this book and my life. We have spent many hours contemplating art and the magic of the Universe and have traveled together to Sweden and Italy. Sasha's *Last Cut* Conversation was the first I did. She spoke of leaving a life in advertising in London for Los Angeles in order to pursue her passion for protecting animals and the earth. In addition to many other talents, Sasha, an accomplished creative director and writer, has a brilliant ability to observe, listen, and magically put perfect words to what she sees and hears, not only in her creative career, but also with every person she encounters in life. She is here to do incredible things for the planet and, in very Sasha fashion, expressed her plans and beliefs eloquently in our *Last Cut* Conversation.

Monique Mitchell and Vanessa Tahay

Get Lit poets Monique Mitchell and Vanessa Tahay bravely and vulnerably shared how reading, writing, and speaking poetry has paved a path to freedom and happiness in their lives. In this raw and moving *Last Cut* Conversation, these two powerful women detailed where they came from and the ways in which they have used their art and voices to cultivate freedom, self-love, empowerment, and joy from pain and hardship. Monique spoke of losing her mother to breast cancer when she was four years old. Vanessa shared of migrating with her family to the United States as a young child and the discrimination and hardship of growing up as a Latinx immigrant in this country. Monique, a poet, *Get Lit* graduate, and now *Get Lit* Head of Community Outreach, and Vanessa, a 2017 Cleveland High graduate and *Get Lit* Classic Slam winner, held nothing back and boldly recited their original poetry at the end of our dialogue. Their raw eloquence and strength give me hope for the future.

For more information on Get Lit, please visit getlit.org, @getlitpoet on Instagram, Twitter, and Facebook. For more information on Monique Mitchell, please visit www. mnqmtchll.com or @mnqmtchll on Instagram and Twitter. For more information on Vanessa Tahay, please visit @vanessa_tahay on Instagram and Twitter or Vanessa Tahay on Facebook.

Get Lit was founded by Diane Luby Lane in 2006 in Los Angeles. Get Lit started in Fairfax and Walt Whitman High Schools and now offers its program in almost one hundred schools. Get Lit–Words Ignite fuses classic and spoken word poetry to increase teen literacy, cultivate enthusiastic learners, and embolden and inspire social consciousness in diverse communities.

Pidgeon Pagonis

I first heard Pidgeon Pagonis's powerful story of growing up intersex through a video clip produced by Human Rights Watch in July 2017. I wanted to learn more about Pidgeon's experience of discovering they were intersex at age nineteen and the subsequent deconstruction of a believed identity, gender, and (false) cancer diagnosis. In our raw, vulnerable *Last Cut* Conversation, Pidgeon discussed a childhood defined by a struggle to conform to a familial and societal definition of "normal." They had been told a believed, yet constructed, story of a childhood cancer diagnosis, built around the notable differences in their body and development as well as the scars on their body. It was not until Pidgeon attended an advanced psychology class in college where the definition of "intersex" was outlined that they discovered they had actually been born with the very condition being taught. Pidgeon underwent three medically unnecessary surgeries at ages one, four, and eleven, as well as years of traumatizing interactions with the medical world. They shared about their rediscovery of self as a non-binary queer activist and filmmaker in the context of reality over protective lies. Pidgeon spoke beautifully to the universal experience of living with trauma and creating a life that feels like one's own.

To connect with Pidgeon Pagonis and learn more about their work, please visit their website, pidgeonismy.name; @pidgeo_n on Instagram; @pidgejen on Twitter; or Pidgeon on Facebook. To view Pidgeon's powerful documentary film The Son I Never Had: Growing Up Intersex, *please contact them directly through their website.*

Josette Tkacik

Ever since I was a child, I have loved to dance. The dance floor has always been a place where I can easily let everything melt away into a state of bliss. As I have gotten older, I have found I can connect with that feeling in a club or at a party, but rarely in a class anymore. Too often the focus is on the mirrors and body image. A few years ago, my dear friend Anne Van de Water invited me to a Zumba class at the local recreation center in Santa Barbara, California. Given my love of dance, I accepted. Yet, I will not lie about the trepidation I had of finding myself among a bunch of women stiffly staring at themselves in a mirror. Josette Tkacik and her Zumba revolution proved me wrong. Her energy blew me away. Josette's Zumba class is nothing reminiscent of any other dance class I have taken. You feel as if you are transported to a dance floor on Ibiza, Spain.

Six days a week, Josette pulls hundreds (yes, hundreds) of people into her classes and leads them through an hour of pure joy and celebration of life. She does this with her expressions and a whistle; not a single word is used during class, and there are no mirrors to be found. Egos and all other life stresses are checked at the door and, honestly, the most diverse group I have seen in Santa Barbara collectively dances together with beaming smiles. What happens in that room is nothing short of magic, but it is also purely the result of what Josette has cultivated in her own life. Diagnosed years ago with mobility-threatening rheumatoid arthritis, Josette, a dancer for life and mother, opted not for a hefty pharmaceutical regimen, but for her own recipe for wellness. She wanted to be healthy and present for her son and found an alternative way to heal. So, instead of leading class with a microphone from a wheelchair, she dances on her feet every night in celebration of her new lease on life. Josette is a medical miracle, and her beauty, wisdom, and joy are contagious.

For more information on Josette Tkacik and her Zumba work, please visit www. josettetkacik.com and @josettetkacik on Instagram.

Ronny Turiaf

When I had my jewelry company, Adesso, I had the pleasure of meeting so many wonderful people. In 2012, I sent jewelry to a stylist for a couple of National Basketball Association (NBA) players. One of them, Ronny Turiaf, loved the pieces, but beyond that, he was moved by my personal story. We had something profound in common. We both were cruising along in our early twenties, feeling healthy and well, when we were told that we were sick inside and needed surgery. I was diagnosed with thyroid cancer at age twenty-one, and Ronny, after being drafted by the Los Angeles Lakers right out of college at age twenty-two, was told he had an enlarged aortic root in his heart that required immediate surgery. There is something life changing in feeling the fullness of your youth and then hearing the shocking news that something you cannot see or feel is about to change your life. After receiving the jewelry, Ronny reached out to me on the phone on his way to the celebratory parade for his NBA Championship win with the Miami Heat. We connected through jewelry and have been dear friends ever since that phone call. In 2016, I had the honor of sitting down with Ronny to talk about his life and vision after retiring from professional basketball a year prior. Our conversation was full of his wisdom and insight about leading a purposeful life according to one's own time and dreams.

For more information on Ronny Turiaf, please visit @ronny_turiaf on Twitter and @ronnyturiaf on Instagram.

Anne Van de Water

I was given the gift of yoga classes with Anne Van de Water for my birthday ten years ago. We first met at her magical home in Santa Barbara just a few months after I had my preventive double mastectomy. I was a relatively new mother and in dire need of some guidance in learning to love and use my body after giving birth and invasive surgery. That gift became one that keeps giving. Our first yoga lesson was the beginning of a deeply supportive and dear friendship. I have had the opportunity to work and play with Anne in many different capacities. She is a powerful life and lifestyle coach, health and wellness practitioner, loyal friend, and incredible travel sidekick. One of the threads that continues to bind not only our working relationship, but also our friendship, is a shared love of the truth. We continue to support each other in showing up in the world in a manner that lines up with our values and beliefs. Having this *Last Cut* Conversation was deeply meaningful for me. Our dialogue touched upon many interesting aspects of relationship and offered a beautiful marker in time for our friendship and lives.

For more information on Anne Van de Water, please visit annevandewater.com and @annevandewater on Instagram, Facebook and Twitter.

Jennifer Yashari

In August 2017, I reunited with my childhood friend Jennifer Yashari, who opened up about living with GNE Myopathy, formerly known as hereditary inclusion body myopathy (HIBM), a rare degenerative disease that causes muscle cells to progressively weaken. Diagnosed in her early thirties, Jennifer, a psychiatrist, has learned to cope with the massive loss delivered with the disease and all the subsequent losses that have come in its wake over time. She started a blog, *Living with HIBM*, in 2011 and writes beautifully and with a piercing rawness about the experience of living with an ever-evolving disability that affects how she moves, parents, and interacts with the world. Jennifer detailed the importance of mourning each and every loss fully, so that we can then do our best to be present in life, and of fostering strong, loving relationships to support us on the ride. In telling her own story, she provided guidance and vision for how to speak with others about differences and how to maintain a connected mindfulness in the process.

For more information on Jennifer Yashari, please visit jenniferyasharimd.com, or her blog, livingwithhibm.com.

thank you

Acknowledgements

Thank you to my body for being my greatest teacher in life. You have provided the blocks and blossoming that have led to my most impactful growth over the years. I appreciate your strength, power, mystery, and ability to heal time and time again.

Thank you to my daughter, Mina, for being another of my monumental teachers in life. My relationship to my body changed through bringing you into this world. You teach me things about myself, love, and growth every single day. I love you to the moon and back and back again infinitely.

Thank you to my mother, Jeanne, for being an infinite fountain of support in all that I do and feel throughout my life. You model generosity in a most profound way. My explant surgery and decision to share this chapter of my life through *Last Cut Project* has pushed the boundaries of our relationship and brought us to a deeper connection and closeness. You have shown me that we all have the capacity to grow and change if there is an earnest willingness to learn and understand. I love you.

Thank you to my dad, Dick, and step-mom, Cameron, for being supportive of my last cut moments over the years. You held my hand the first time I saw my chest after my double mastectomy and supported me without question when I said I wanted my implants removed. I love you both.

Thank you to my siblings, Alan, Maril and Blake Davis, and their mates, Matt

Roberts and Melissa Clark, for loving and supporting me throughout the years, phases and last cuts. From bowl cuts to last cuts, I love you.

Thank you to my sweet grandparents, Mildred, Morris, Anne and Alfred. I am rooted by your legacy. You live on in my heart and actions.

Thank you to my stepfather, Don. Though you are no longer alive in this dimension, I feel your presence always. You continue to inspire my truth, self-expression and humor. I miss you and carry you with me.

Thank you to Lisa Field, *Last Cut Project* photographer and dear friend, for agreeing to embark on this wild documentary journey within moments of my decision to have the explant surgery. Your eye and heart have made a permanent imprint on me and *Last Cut Project*. You brought more than your camera to all of our time together over the years during which *Last Cut Project* was birthed. Your willingness to stay in the room; to ask the questions and be present for the answers; to hold me in moments of pain, healing, growth, and joy; to listen to me ask (over and over again), "Is there value in my having you take pictures of me for public con-

sumption?"; and to evolve with me in friendship and art has been second to none. Together we have rewritten and relearned. We have shared creativity and rebuilt trust. I could not have done this without you. Hearts and squares forever.

Thank you to Anne Van de Water for being a fellow lover of the truth and for showing up consistently as my rock and sidekick in learning, traveling, and exploring the depth within and out in the world. You have been present for my most significant last cuts in the last ten years. You ask the right questions, offer steady presence, and hold me accountable to our shared dedication to change and growth. Here's to this lifetime and all the others we have shared.

Thank you to Susan Nichols for always bringing the ethereal and the real. You have introduced me to some of the paths that have led to my deepest healing. You model softness and strength like no other. Thank you for always holding the highest vision for every outcome.

Thank you to Janelle Odair for being a beacon of information about the research on silicone implants. You were the bearer of news I needed to hear in perfect, divine timing. My explant and the birth of *Last Cut Project* happened with the grace of your suggestion to read and look into the impact of my implants on my health. My heart holds a fountain of gratitude for you.

Thank you to Marni Caputo for holding my hand when I heard the words "The tumor is malignant" twenty-two years ago and for holding my history from the day we met at Tufts University. Your presence is lasting and forever in my heart. I feel you and Tim with me always.

Thank you to Monique Mitchell for coming into my life and lighting it up in a most profound way. I have infinite appreciation for your being one of the first to read and provide feedback on the *Last Cut Project* book draft. Your wisdom and insight enrich my world and Mina's. You are poetry in all you do and all that you bring to those you encounter.

Thank you to Talila Gafter for always asking the pointed philosophical questions that make me think. You inspire me to go deeper with your thought and discipline. I am grateful for your friendship and support.

Thank you to Ronny Turiaf for always asking me the deep questions that encourage me in my personal growth and for inspiring me to be the most authentic version of myself. I will forever be grateful for your willingness to follow the white rabbits and offer support in the claiming and clearing along the way. Your presence in my life is a gift.

Thank you to my amazing crew of friends, supporters and cheerleaders from these past few years: Carrie Hoffman, Sarah Clark, Elizabeth Colling, Leah and Mark Watson, Peter and Pieter Crawford-van Meeuwen, Justine and Josiah Hamilton, Erika Paulson, Rob Bourdon, Annie Hawkins, Leonard Marks, Dayle Zukor, Leslie Rottman, Scott Brown, Marco Orsi, Jacopo de Bertoldi, Ella Gafter, Merryl Brown, Whitney Goodman, Jameela Pedicini, Ariel Osterweis, Sasha Markova, Mariel Osborn, Brett Tyne, Sophie Milner, Jonas Milner, Renee Stahl Dektor, Kelly Macías, Melinda Alexander, Zoë Buckman, Sophia Bush, Alejandro Ameijeiras, Janice Muscio, Rachel Brown, Mali Milenbaugh, Ayda Robana, Melissa Bishop, Shadow and Angie Seacliff, Karin Pine, Ellen Sandler, Shelley Limpert, Kara Slater, Adam Lipsic, Emily Chung, Alice Van de Water, Marandah and Gibson Field-Elliot and Berta Rojo.